Soldiers and Sled Dogs

Soldiers & Sled Dogs

A History of Military Dog Mushing

Charles L. Dean

UNIVERSITY OF NEBRASKA PRESS
LINCOLN & LONDON

Library of Congress
Cataloging-in-Publication Data
Dean, Charles L.
Soldiers and sled dogs:
a history of military dog mushing
/ Charles L. Dean.
p.   cm.
Includes bibliographical
references and index.
ISBN 0-8032-1728-5 (cloth: alk. paper)
1. Dogs—War use—United States.
2. Dogs—War use.
3. Sled dogs—United States.
4. Sled dogs. 5. Dogsledding—United States.
6. Dogsledding. I. Title.
UH100.D37   2005
355.4'24—dc22
2005015601

To the men and dogs who
served in the cold and ice
defending the far frontiers of
their empires, so they will not
fade from memory like their
tracks in the snow.

To Catherine, who has shared
the cold, the snow, and the
dogs with me.

and

To Akla, Tara, Chukchi,
Queenie, Chinook, Bandit,
Yukon, and Nikki: they taught
us more than we could ever
teach them.

In a world where the forms of transportation have been brought to a high state of perfection, where the airplane is fast supplanting other methods of travel, there is still a place for the use of sledge dogs.

—FM 25–6, Dog Transportation

Contents

Illustrations

Preface

While serving in Alaska over twenty years ago as an "Arctic expert" at the Northern Warfare Training Center, I ran across an old field manual on dog transportation. I quickly perused it and noted that the U.S. Army had at one time used enough sled dogs to warrant a field manual. I reshelved the book in the school's library and forgot it for almost sixteen years. Toward the end of my tour of duty in Alaska, I became more aware of northern-breed dogs and the sport of dog mushing when local news coverage of the fledgling Iditarod race piqued my interest. Until then my only exposure to northern dogs and dogsleds was watching the Saturday morning television serial *Sergeant Preston of the Yukon* and having to memorize Robert Service's poem "The Cremation of Sam McGee" in grammar school.

After I left both Alaska and the army, my new bride Catherine and I settled in Colorado. Not long after we moved to a small log cabin in a mountain community, Catherine wanted a dog, particularly a Siberian husky. We both loved climbing and skiing, and she thought a husky would fit our lifestyle well. Akla was our first sled dog. He was descended from a dog owned by Leonard Seppala (a famous Alaskan sled dog racer), with the traits of a wolf: long legs, heavy fur, sable coloring, and an independent "hammerhead" demeanor. We trained him to pull us on skis—skijoring, as it is called in Europe. Actually, he trained us to ride behind him at breakneck speeds through timber and rocks on narrow, steep mountain trails. It was not long before we wanted another dog so both of us could skijor. One thing led to another, and we put together our first small recreational dog team. It changed our life forever. As for sled dog people everywhere, dogs became the focus of every day.

This book grew out of that whole sequence. My love for the dogs combined with my interest in military history started me on a search for information on the military use of dog teams. Much to my disappointment, I found there was very little material on the subject, and what there was did not go into detail. The use of dog teams within the military was very limited in number and in scope, and official records hardly exist. My search began. This book is the result of almost five years of research. I have tried not only to include a broad history of military mushing but also to describe in accurate detail the personalities, equipment, techniques, and color of the various eras and places. Field manual *FM 25-6, Dog Transportation* (1944) was a source for the day-to-day procedures used by U.S. Army dog drivers. It is amazing how little has changed in almost a hundred years of the bond between sled dogs and their soldier drivers.

Since I was not there to witness events or talk to many of the participants, I have also incorporated the research of others. The notes and bibliography list my sources and give credit to all these people. To make the book less "scholarly" and easier to read, I have gathered widely scattered and little-known information about military dog driving and tied it together with official facts drawn from previously undiscovered military and private documents as well as personal accounts and other published works. Photographs are products of their times, and many of those in the book are copies of copies given to me by veterans or their families. Many of these photos were probably taken by professionals, from the Signal Corps or otherwise, with copies given to the subjects, as was the practice. Thus most photographs are credited not to the unknown photographer but to the contributor. Sometimes poor-quality contemporary snapshots are the only known photos of the events or equipment being depicted. Most of Otto Schulz's personal photographs showing German canine operations were destroyed after the war, for fear of reprisals against the families of former ss soldiers still living in the Occupied Soviet Zone in Germany. There are few photographs available anywhere of actual search and rescue operations conducted by U.S. dog teams. Photographs taken by participants were confiscated at the time. It was considered not in the best interests of the war effort to depict Allied dead and wounded, or even aircraft crashes.

As with the photographs, the wording of my sources also reflects the times, since much of the information came from previously published material as well as official documentation. As an example, the word *Eskimo* is used to describe the native Arctic peoples instead of the modern, more correct, term *Inuit*. Spelling is also derived from the same documents and reflects this earlier era. For example, for the native sled *qamutik* I use the previously accepted spelling *komatik*. The terms *sled* and *sledge* are used interchangeably, since the difference is often regional. Some make the distinction that a sled is ridden by the driver and a sledge is not. *Sled* is a more recent general term.

During my research and writing I came in contact with many extremely interesting people who lived the history I have recorded. As the project unfolded, I wished I had started a few years sooner, since many key people had died before I began my endeavor. Stuart A. Mace was one of those. Much of the information in this book centers on this man, who was involved throughout the development of military dog team transportation during World War II. He was present at Camp Hale, Camp Rimini, and Fort Robinson. Several of those I talked with are quickly fading into the twilight, along with their accounts and remembrances. A line from Jack London's story "The White Silence" aptly describes these men: "Those of the Northland are early taught the futility of words and the inestimable value of deeds." They were all men of action, with little time to record their doings. I hope that the written words of this book will remain as a tribute both to them and to their dogs. The actions and deeds are their history; the compilation of words is mine.

Acknowledgments

History generally gets recorded after the events themselves occur. The historian frequently is not a participant, most often attempting to assemble the story of happenings long past and forgotten. This book is chiefly a compilation of information drawn from those who took part in the events I describe, and I could not have written it without their help. During the five years of research before writing, I asked many people for information, photographs, and leads. To all of them I offer my sincere thanks, since even the smallest bit of knowledge often led to a mother lode. Others became extremely interested and helpful. I am indebted to these people, who became friends: David W. Armstrong Jr., a World War II dog driver, is a walking encyclopedia about military sled dogs. He is the prime mover for a military mushing museum in Helena, Montana. Dave was as enthusiastic about the project as I was. He not only answered questions in many letters and phone calls but let me use his unpublished memoirs. The technical information on military sleds was made possible by the help of John A. Matovich of Malta, Montana, who either built or supervised the building of almost every sled produced by the U.S. Army during World War II. Lynne Mace (daughter of Stuart A. Mace), of Toklat Galleries in Ashcroft, Colorado, gave me free access to family records and photographs. Fortunately for history, Stuart had kept invaluable information from his army service with sled and pack dogs. His interest in photography and his love of sled dogs led to many of the photos in this book. Lynne made available much rich detail of that era. The chapter on German Nordic-style dogsledding could not have been written without Hans Burtscher of Bludenze, Austria, a World War II Gebirgsjaeger veteran, and Otto Schulz of Ried am Inn, Austria. Otto is the only surviving dog driver from the Sixth ss Gebirgs Division (NORD). His recollections and diary were priceless in recreating that relatively unknown portion of history. Eugene Armstrong of Colorado Springs, Colorado, and Francis M. Dawdy, of Garland, Texas, both retired U.S. Air Force pararescuemen, gave me invaluable postwar information on parachuting sled dogs. Thanks to Judy Ferguson of Delta Junction, Alaska, for use of her research and audiotapes of interviews with Jesse Taylor concerning sled dog operations at the Army Arctic Indoctrination School. Poul Ipsen of the Danish Sledge Patrol SIRIUS in Greenland contributed photographs as well as sharing his expertise. I received information on the Italian sled dogs in World War I, as well as photographs of them, from Silverio Vecchio of the Centro Studi, Associazione Nazionale Alpini, and from John Ceruti of the Museo della Guerra Bianca, Temú, Italy. These people are not professional archivists or employed by the government to assist researchers. They contributed because they too wanted the history of military dog mushing preserved. My sincerest gratitude to you all.

My heartfelt thanks to my wife Catherine for her support, encouragement, and assistance. As a former army officer herself, she was able to help translate my technical military style of writing to something more palatable to civilian readers.

1. Sled Dogs Supply Soldiers

Alaska to the Alps

Though sled dogs have been helping humans since they were first tamed and broken to the trace thousands of years ago, their history of supporting soldiers is much more recent. Most of that support can be traced back to the U.S. Army's involvement in Alaska in the early 1900s and to Europeans' efforts to use dogs on both the Western and Alpine fronts during World War I.

"Seward's Folly" was a vast and capricious land. As military presence in Alaska grew, local sourdoughs and Indians provided much information about the vagaries of land and weather. The military soon learned that moving troops in winter was virtually impossible without dog teams, and military outposts began using them as winter transport, mostly hiring local teams and drivers on contract. This method was easier and more cost-effective than attempting to set up a military operation.

Billy Mitchell, who later became known as the father of the U.S. Air Force, was sent to Alaska in 1901 as a young lieutenant to supervise establishment of the Washington–Alaska Military Cable and Telegraph System. When he arrived at Fort Egbert (in eastern Alaska near Eagle), hardly any work was being done on the telegraph system. Troops had been using horses to haul equipment for the project in the summer months, but during the long, brutal winters all work essentially ceased.

Lieutenant Mitchell had been given a deadline of five years to complete an extremely difficult section of line stretched from the Canadian border to Valdez on the coast and Tanana in the interior. Being innovative in solving problems in Alaska, just as he was later when he proved that the flimsy aircraft of the day could sink a battleship, he consulted local civilian and native populations. He devised a plan to use dog teams to move equipment and supplies into place during the winter when the ground was frozen. With

FIGURE 1.1. Soldiers and sled dogs at Fort Egbert, Alaska, about 1902.
(Eagle Historical Society, Eagle City, Alaska)

all supplies in position, work on the telegraph line could move along uninterrupted during the long days of summer.[1]

Mitchell was the first military leader to purchase sled dogs and keep them year round instead of relying on seasonal contracts. Following the advice of the locals, Mitchell soon became an expert at selecting sled dogs. Before long he had acquired two hundred dogs, which he kept in a corral at Fort Egbert, running loose in a huge pack.[2] This is contrary to today's standard practice, in which dogs are kept individually chained.

One of the best dogs Mitchell acquired was a Mackenzie River husky named Pointer, who weighed about 120 pounds. "The dog was so fierce," Mitchell said, "that I had to cut off his fangs to keep him from killing the other dogs."[3] This was a common practice among the Alaskan Eskimos, as reported by the Czechoslovakian explorer Ian Wetzl: "At six months of age wolf pups that had been taken from their parents had their incisors pulled, filed, or broken off. After being castrated also, the dogs were then trained to the trace."[4] After losing his fangs, Pointer became "tremendously attached" to Mitchell and eventually became his best lead dog.[5]

Mitchell credits Pointer with saving his life on numerous occasions when he broke through river ice. Mitchell said, "Pointer was so strong that if he could get his front feet on anything solid, he could pull the next dog out and then the next."[6] One day while scouting the telegraph route, with the ambient temperature hovering at minus sixty degrees Fahrenheit, Lieutenant Mitchell broke through thin ice and fell into icy water up to his shoulders as Pointer struggled to pull the entire team free. Many a musher and dog team have perished when ice fractured beneath them.

Mitchell used many dog handling techniques common to the indigenous peoples of Alaska. Removing incisors was one. Another technique was to use a twenty-foot whip to keep order among the team. He would even stand by with his whip during feeding time to ensure that no dog would steal the others' food or start a fight.[7]

Mitchell initially trained two good dog teams so that he and a companion could scout the proposed route of the telegraph line. During this reconnaissance, Mitchell learned what the dogs could do. He also learned that, contrary to expectations, men could work in the extreme cold of Alaska's winter. After Mitchell's survey trip, teams of men and dogs were put to work in earnest moving cables, poles, and other equipment. The stalled telegraph line was completed in only two years, three years ahead of the original schedule,[8] largely because of Mitchell's foresight.

During the Alaskan gold rush from 1898 to 1906, dog teams were the primary method of hauling freight throughout the region. Dog teams were hitched to sleds during the winter. In summer they were hitched to small trams on rails, to carts, and even to barges that they pulled along streams. So many people were using dogs throughout this boisterous era that high-stakes gambling for gold soon spawned wagering on dog races and freight-pulling contests. These races continued long after the gold strike ended. The All-Alaska Sweepstakes, which became known internationally, was the most famous, and many competitors became known throughout the world. Scotty Allan won the All-Alaska three times as well as placing second three times and third twice. Explorers such as Roald Amundsen and Vilhjalmur Stefansson asked him for advice about their upcoming Arctic explorations.[9] During World War I, foreign military powers sought his expertise.

During the Great War in Europe from 1914 to 1918, all combatants used dogs in many roles. The French and Belgian armies used draught dogs to pull carts of supplies and ammunition as well as to transport wounded soldiers.

French and German soldiers met in combat in the Vosges Mountains on the Western Front during the severe winter of 1914–15. Much of the fighting was done on skis, and deep snow made it hard to supply soldiers with food and ammunition. [10]

A French army captain named Mufflet, who had been to Alaska during the gold rush, suggested using dog teams in the Vosges to move freight over the snow. The French government asked Scotty Allan to supply dogs and sleds and to train soldiers in dog driving. [11]

For this mission, Allan purchased 106 dogs around Nome. To transport them to a barge that would take them to the cargo ship anchored offshore, Allan tied all the dogs to one long rope like a gang line. He attached this rope to a team of horses and a wagon to supply braking power. He put a good lead dog in front, and the world's longest dog team proceeded without incident to the barge, where the dogs were loaded for the first leg of their journey to France, along with sleds, harnesses, and two tons of dried fish. [12]

After docking in Vancouver, the Alaskan dogs were transported in secrecy across Canada on a guarded railroad train. Three hundred more dogs from Canada and the Arctic joined the original Alaskan group in Quebec. Sixty more sleds and 350 dog harnesses had been made and added to the shipment. The next problem was how to ship over 400 dogs across the Atlantic, which was infested with German submarines. The ship's captain did not want any dogs on deck because their noise might alert enemy subs to the ship's position, but Allan trained the dogs not to sing or bark during the two-week passage. The dogs were housed in shipping crates chained to the deck, which served as dog kennels at the front. [13]

Once he arrived in the mountains of France, Allan's next task was to train fifty Chasseurs Alpins, French mountain soldiers, to drive the dogs. These soldiers and dogs were under the command of the French lieutenant René Hass, with Allan acting as technical adviser, and the men had to overcome the language barrier, learning English dog commands. Training went extremely well except for one enormous dogfight that involved piles of fighting dogs up to six feet deep. Less than two months after leaving Nome, dog teams with French drivers were hauling supplies and ammunition to areas that previously could not be reached. One group of these dogs delivered ninety tons of ammunition to an artillery battery in only four days. It had taken up to two weeks for a combination of men, horses, and mules to accomplish the same thing. Columns of dog teams often stretched over a mile. Allan noted that "the soldiers acted more like it was play than work, even whooping and hollering in attempts to pass each other."[14] On another mission, dogs assisted in laying over eighteen miles of field telephone wire in one night, allowing a totally isolated unit of soldiers to communicate with headquarters again.[15]

When the mountain snows melted, dogs were hitched to cars on a narrow-gauge railway that had been laid to continue transport of supplies and munitions. The cost of their upkeep was small, since plenty of horse flesh was available from the slaughter of combat. Dogs were eminently more economical than horses. Two seven-dog teams could do the work of five horses in the formidable terrain.

Three Alaskan sled dogs in French service were awarded the Croix de Guerre, one of France's highest military honors, for their actions in combat. Details of their deeds are not available, but after the war, all the dogs who worked with the Chasseurs Alpins were rewarded with a life of leisure for their heroic service to their adopted country. They were released from service and became pets in France's Alpine tourist region.[16]

World War I is well remembered for the massive carnage on the Western Front. Less universally recognized is the difficult fighting between the Italian and Austro-Hungarian armies that took place in brutal mountain conditions on the Alpine Front. In one remote area, regional operations were carried out around Mount Adamello in the Trentino salient. Fighting at altitudes ranging from 10,200 to 11,500 feet. Battles occurred over a long period (1914–18), in terrain that was considered almost impossible for any military engagement. Military historians consider this combat "unique in the annals of mountain warfare."[17] Severe winter conditions combined with the altitude made troop supply one of the greatest challenges for military commanders.

Pian di Neve was a glacier that surrounded an area of the Tonale Pass at 6,108 feet. This glacier was a key location for the Italian Alpini (mountain troops) who fought here. Horses and mules replaced the men who originally carried supplies across the glacier, five miles round trip. But these animals could not cope with the extremely severe weather, which dropped up to thirteen feet of snow. Dog teams eventually replaced them for this arduous task. Dogs transported three tons of provisions and nearly ten tons of firewood daily during the last two years of World War I to supply the four thousand men fighting in this hostile region.[18]

The project of using dogs to transport provisions was started by the Milan kennel club. Sanitary corpsmen helping to move wounded soldiers from the front had proposed using dogs: the kennel club established a committee to procure them, and experiments were conducted as early as 1915. As in France, there were no northern breed sled dogs available, but Italy recruited dogs from the surrounding countryside instead of bringing them in from elsewhere. Some were even enlisted from southern Italy. Ultimately 250 shepherds' dogs were trained as sled dogs in military kennels at Bologna. Various breeds including Saint Bernards were purchased for twenty to thirty lire each. Dogs had to be ten months to three years old and needed heavy coats. White coloring was desirable for camouflage on snow. All dogs had a serial number tattooed inside an ear, but most handlers also gave them names. Dogs were so well disciplined that they could be fed in two parallel rows facing each other. Their food was placed in bowls between the rows, and they would not budge from their position of "attention" until a bugle was sounded. To prevent fights, dogs were trained not to invade another dog's space during feeding time. In the mountains dogs received the same rations as Alpini soldiers: bread and meat in the morning and bread at the evening meal.[19]

Teams of two or three dogs wearing leather harnesses were attached to sleds by wooden shafts. The *cagnari* (as dog drivers were called) used skis or walked alongside their dogs instead of riding the sled as the French did, imitating Alaskan mushing. The center dog was considered the lead dog. This hitch was called a troika after the Russian three-horse configuration. Sleds were similar in design to Antarctic sleds but were simpler in construction, with blunt rear ends. A brake consisting of a wooden board pierced with iron spikes was attached to the rear with chains. *Cagnari* could step on it with both feet for maximum braking on glacier ice. Sleds were used to transport both men and material; there was even a group of sled-stretchers for evacuating the wounded. Italian dog teams made three trips across the glacier each day to supply troops, with only one day of rest each week. Each team towed a sled loaded with 120 to 140 pounds of cargo.[20]

The main kennel, at Garibaldi Pass on Mandrone Glacier in the Adamello Group, housed two hundred dogs. It was a wooden shack built on a concrete slab raised three feet off the snow for insulation. Dogs rested on straw in compartments off a central corridor. Another group of forty dogs kept in a forward area at Passo Lobbia Althpar was used to supply advances in troop

FIGURE I.2. "Troika" with *cagnari* near Garibaldi Pass (10,450 feet) on Mandrone Glacier in the Adamello Group. (Photo by Captain Doctor Carcano. Museo della Guerra Bianca, Adamello records, Temú-Italia-Carc-67)

lines. There was also a small collection center for injured and ill dogs in the bottom of the Valley d'Avio, near the village of Temú where dogs could rest, acclimate, and heal before being sent back to the front lines.[21]

One Alpini officer described dogs in action as "wonderful, robust, and intelligent animals," eager to work. They departed on each supply trek as soon as the sled was barely loaded. Dogs would trot on moderate terrain, but on steeper sections they would slow to a walk and lower their heads to pull. Teams were even credited with spoiling Austrian ambushes by barking when they encountered unfamiliar smells on the wind.[22]

Italian sled dogs served loyally and gallantly throughout 1917–18, and many were lost to enemy artillery fire. Just before the armistice ending the Great War, the Austrians hastily left the glacier district with the Italian Alpine Corps in pursuit. In the soldiers' haste to end the war, all the dogs were abandoned and forgotten at Temú. Hungry and thirsty, they reverted to the wild for survival. Finally they became a threat to local civilians. Unlike Scotty Allan's huskies that were rewarded for their duty in France, the faithful Italian Alpine sled dogs ended their military service without recognition or reward. Because there was a meat shortage in the mountains, they were eventually hunted to extinction, and most ended up in the stew pot.[23]

The U.S. Army made no use of sled dogs during World War I. With the exception of a regiment of American troops dispatched into northern Russia (North Russia Expeditionary Force) in 1918–19, it was not engaged in combat in areas where dogs might have proved useful. By contrast, the British Army, which was in overall command of the international force in northern Russia and Siberia, used Canadian dog teams with Canadian soldier-drivers attached to the Royal Army Medical Corps (RAMC). The dogs were "usefully employed in drawing stretchers with wounded from the firing line."[24] These Canadian huskies served the British forces around Murmansk and Archangel in combat against the Bolshevik army. As was true for other combatants during the Great War who used sled dogs, the evacuation of wounded proved one of the most important tasks of the Canadian sled teams in northern Russia. The sleds used were lightweight, double-ended Nansen types, called Shackleton sleighs by the English, capable of carrying 800–1,000 pounds as well as a four-stanchion basket type freight sled.[25] Some Shackleton sleighs were even fitted with removable combined handlebars and side rails. Both sled versions were equipped with springboard brakes. Like most freight sleds of the era, neither allowed the driver to comfortably stand on the runners and ride. Dogs were attached to the sleds in either a four-dog tandem configuration of a seven-dog double tandem (Nome hitch). Harnesses were leather "horse collar" design.

After the war, sled dogs were still maintained in Alaska, even during austere times when the military defense budget was drastically cut. There were still a few army dog teams in Alaska during the 1920s and 1930s, years when the army slaughtered horses because if lacked funds to feed them. It had been proved over the years that in Alaska's snow dog teams were the only dependable transportation.

In 1926 the U.S. War Department published a technical regulation concerning dog transportation. It was a forerunner of later field manuals published in 1941 and 1944. The regulation, TR 1380–20, was definitive. It stated that dog transportation "is of great value in countries where snow and ice conditions and lack of roads preclude the use of the horse or mule or motorized transportation."

This regulation defined types of dog teams as heavy and light. Heavy transportation was used to carry men and supplies. Loads were not to exceed the total weight of the dogs minus the weight of the driver. These teams could travel from two and a half to three miles an hour for eight hours. Light transportation, also called messenger transportation, was designed for fast travel in emergencies or for speedy communication. Teams for light transportation could travel at five to six miles an hour for eight hours with a load of no more than twenty-five pounds per dog.[26] These classifications remained standard throughout the entire period of military use of sled dogs. Recommended speeds and load-carrying capacities changed slightly over the years.

The command "Mush!" was an official term designated in the original 1926 technical regulation defining dog training and commands.[27] In later years this term lost favor with army dog drivers. The 1941 version of the manual substituted "All Right!" and stated that it was preferable to "Mush!" However, "Mush!" was still favored by Alaskan dog freighters when the last manual was published in 1944.[28]

For use in Alaska the technical regulation highly recommended two specific dog breeds: the Mackenzie River husky and the Kobuk Valley dog.[29] The Mackenzie River husky was finally recognized toward the end of World War II in attempts to breed the ideal Army transportation dog. The regulation also mentioned malamutes and Siberian huskies as being suited for the area. These were the primary dogs used during World War II.

Various types of sleds were also defined by this technical regulation. The three basic types included one modeled on an Alaskan freight sled that was thirteen feet in overall length, a small eight-foot messenger basket-type sled, and a smaller freight sled ten feet, three inches long that could be used as a trailer or hooked in tandem to increase the load-carrying capacity.[30] Sled design remained unchanged through the publication period of FM 25–6, *Basic Field Manual, Dog Team Transportation* (1941).

In 1938, twenty years after the Armistice ended World War I, a team

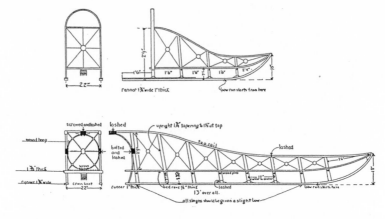

FIGURE 1.3. Comparison of eight-foot messenger sled (*top*) and thirteen-foot freight sled as shown in War Department *Technical Regulation No. 1380-20, Dog Transportation*, June 15, 1926.

consisting of descendants from Scotty Allan's heroic huskies was called back into the French army by the war minister. This dog team helped Lieutenant Flotard (an Alpine soldier and instructor at the Military High Mountain School) and with his comrade Paul-Émile Victor complete a winter traverse of the Alps. Their trek from Nice to Chamonix by the *haute route* (high road of the Alps) was considered quite a feat. During this military exercise, they navigated rigorous obstacles including a dozen steep gorges and nine mountain ridges. When the dogs arrived in Chamonix they were celebrated as heroes. The classic winter traverse received considerable publicity both within France and internationally. Here again in the Alps it was proved that sled dogs could pull heavily loaded sleds where mules with similar loads could not go in winter.[31] Only a few years later, the U.S. Army learned this fact again at Camp Hale, Colorado.

When the Japanese bombed Pearl Harbor on December 7, 1941, there were only fifty sled dogs left in the U.S. Army in Alaska.[32] The few men who drove them represented the paramount military authority on dog transportation at the time. But when the army expanded its sled dog operations, these were not the people consulted. Those who took part in polar expeditions were summoned for their knowledge. Several factors contributed to this oversight.

It occurred partly because New England, where dog racing was popular, was close to Washington DC, and it was partly influenced by individuals like Admiral Richard E. Byrd. Also, the army in Alaska was not considered to be at the forefront of recognition, innovation, or modernization. Alaska was not a career-building assignment for officers. Being assigned there was considered banishment from the mainstream.

The modern mechanized military judged dog teams, like horses, to be antiquated. Then it rediscovered sled dogs' unsurpassed capability for traversing ice and unbroken snow, the terrain that encompassed almost 45 percent of the North American landmass and nearly 65 percent of that of Eurasia. This part of the world became an important consideration in the truly global conflict of World War II and its aftermath, the cold war.

2. Sled Dogs Enter the Service

Chinook Kennels, New Hampshire

Chinook Kennels can be considered the birthplace of U.S. military dogsledding. The kennels are in Wonalancet, New Hampshire, nestled at the edge of the White Mountains, an area ideal for raising and training sled dogs. It was here that true military use of sled dogs became a reality in the early years of World War II. Dog drivers, trainers, kennel masters, and even the dogs simultaneously became government issue (GI) when Chinook Kennels was selected by the Quartermaster Corps to provide dogs and troops for military operations.

Although the army had used dogs in Alaska as far back as the early 1900s, they had been hired on contract with local drivers for specific needs and a limited time. But as far back as June 15, 1926, a War Department technical regulation (no. 1380–20) stated that dogs could be purchased with military funds requested from the Quartermaster General through proper channels. All requests had to include the average market price for sled dogs in the area where they were needed. Once the request was approved, dogs could be bought on the open market. It was at Chinook Kennels that such purchases began to be made in significant numbers.

Arthur Walden, the founder of Chinook Kennels, had been to Alaska in 1896 during the gold rush and had used dog teams to move freight. Walden became adept at this method of travel, and when he returned to New Hampshire he decided to acquire several dogs for a team of his own. One was a large yellow mixed breed of mastiff descent, which he bred to a descendant of one of Admiral Robert E. Peary's Greenland huskies. The resulting breed of sled dog became known for its tremendous power and endurance and its friendly disposition. Walden named one of the pups Chinook,[1] after the lead dog (a half-breed Mackenzie River husky)[2] he'd had to leave behind in

Alaska. Walden continued breeding these dogs for many years and called the breed Chinooks.

Chinook was an exceptional lead dog. The team he led would respond when Walden stood on his porch and gave them commands as they worked out in the field. Walden and his team became the impetus for New England dogsled racing, and in 1924 he founded the New England Sled Dog Club. Walden won many races during this era and also drove a dog team to the summit of Mount Washington (the highest point in New Hampshire), a feat unknown in those days.[3]

Because of his reputation in New England, in 1928 Walden was accepted as lead dog driver and trainer for Admiral Richard E. Byrd's Antarctic expedition. For a year he procured and trained dogs, assisted by Norman D. Vaughn, Freddy Crockett, and Eddie Goodale.[4] These men would all later become military dog drivers, renowned for using dog teams to find and rescue pilots downed during World War II.

When they arrived in Antarctica, dogs were immediately put to work. All the teams broke numerous records for amount of weight per load and number of loads carried. Walden's lead dog, Chinook, pulled freight on the expedition even though he was over twelve years old by this time. At some point Chinook wandered off and was never found, echoing his tribal ancestry.[5]

Before leaving for Antarctica, Walden went into partnership with Mr. and Mrs. Milton J. Seeley, whom he had met in 1924 when they purchased a pup from him. In 1928 they moved to Wonalancet. Seeley, a chemist, developed a better diet to sustain dogs during the rigors of the upcoming Antarctic expedition. Though Seeley's formula was never patented, it was the basis for modern commercial dog foods.

The Seeleys supervised the kennels while Walden was at the South Pole. When he returned, Walden sold them the entire operation. The Seeleys' devotion to sled dogs established them as the primary authority within the United States on all sled dog breeds, particularly Siberian huskies and Alaskan malamutes. As a result, the Seeleys trained and supplied all the dogs for subsequent Byrd Antarctic expeditions. Becoming close friends with the admiral, they ultimately built an entrenched reputation as sled dog experts.[6]

In 1942 the Quartermaster Corps selected Chinook Kennels to procure dogs and drivers for military operations. There were many reasons for this choice. Paramount were the Seeleys' expertise and reputation, as well as their

FIGURE 2.1. Military sled dogs in training at Chinook Kennels. Old automobile chassis were used in place of sleds when there was no snow. This became a standard training technique. (U.S. Army Military History Institute)

friendship with Byrd. In addition, New England had become the nucleus of recreational dogsledding at a national level. Many people who had worked with Seeley during the Byrd expeditions kept in touch with him years later, so Seeley was able to refer the Army Personnel Section to men who had experience with sled dogs. Several of them had already been drafted, including David W. Armstrong Jr., Robert W. Brown, and Garfield W. Dicey. All three were first transferred from their current military assignments to Eastern Remount Headquarters at Front Royal, Virginia, then sent to Chinook Kennels in October 1942. The military men were quartered with local residents and ate their meals at a boardinghouse, since no military housing was available. Richard S. Moulton had also been drafted into the army when he returned from the 1939 Byrd expedition. He had originally been assigned to Baffin Land but was later sent to Chinook Kennels, where he had spent several years preparing dogs for Antarctic expeditions before his own trip to the South Pole. With all his experience, Moulton was put in charge of men and dogs at the kennel. Several months later he was assigned to the

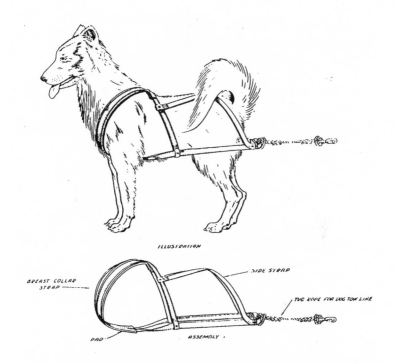

ILLUSTRATION

BREAST COLLAR
STRAP

SIDE STRAP

TUG ROPE FOR DOG TOW LINE

PAD

ASSEMBLY

FIGURE 2.2. U.S. Army "Siwash" dog harness as shown in Jefferson Quartermaster Depot Specification 387, August 18, 1943. The official designation was "harness, sled dog, shoulder strap type." It was originally developed at Chinook Kennels.

same job at Camp Rimini, Montana, which was just being established by the Quartermaster General.[7]

As the number of dogs at the kennel grew, training became more innovative. Lacking snow, men used stripped Austin automobile chassis to train teams. Dogs were assembled into teams as soon as they arrived. One matched team of eight light yellow huskies became known as the Cream Team: Jack, Jill Jr., Saucey, Darkar, Noel, Nome, Mala, and Jill Sr. The Cream Team was trained by David Armstrong, then shipped to Camp Rimini, Montana, and later to Camp Hale, Colorado. Another team of Siberian husky littermates put together by Robert Brown included General, Colonel, Major, Captain, Lieutenant, Sergeant, Corporal, and Private. These eight-dog teams were based on an army conception that teams should consist of seven dogs and

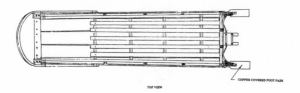

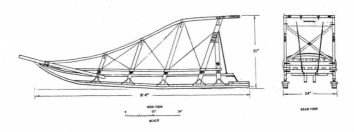

FIGURE 2.3. Plan of Wonalancet sled. In deep snow, the sled was supposed to float on the toboggan bottom. (Illustration by author)

one spare,[8] a standard later replaced by eight dogs and one spare.[9] Since there was never a "spare," in reality it was a team of nine.

Decisions that Seeley and other kennel employees made during this period affected the entire army sled dog program. Dog team standardization was one area of consequence. Another was equipment. Most equipment was chosen and procured based on successful use during the U.S. Antarctic expedition. The low-back draft harness that became standard military issue was refined from the original Chinook Kennels design. Known as the Siwash harness, this pattern was extensively tested by Russians on Dickson Island in Siberia as well as by Byrd's explorers in Antarctica.[10] The harness was constructed of one-inch-wide military cotton webbing and padded with half-inch-thick wool felt, both sewn and riveted together at all stress points. The neck yoke design placed most of the strain of pulling on the dog's chest and shoulders. It used a wooden spreader bar to prevent side traces from chafing the dogs' flanks. All harnesses were handmade and individually sized.

The sled used extensively at Chinook was the basis for most sleds developed and built later by the military during World War II. It was a five-stanchion combination sled and toboggan, originally built near the kennels by Arthur King and called the Wonalancet sled after the town.[11] Since it had been used successfully in the Antarctic, it was initially considered ideal for military use with dogs. But as the sled was more widely used in the deep snows of the Rocky Mountains, it proved less than adequate.[12]

Chinook Kennels had its own military veterinarian assigned by the Remount Division. Because he had experience working with the kennel vet, David Armstrong was assigned to assist the new man. By reputation the new vet was the "best mule man in the army," but it quickly became evident that his experience with dogs was limited. When he spayed the females on Armstrong's Cream Team, he did not use enough sedation. Armstrong had to administer ether in addition to the Nembutal the vet had given. Since he was used to larger animals, his surgical incisions were four inches long instead of the usual inch and a half. After Mr. Seeley made serious complaints to the Remount Division, a small-animal vet was sent to replace the mule doctor.[13]

Most dog team training was done about six miles from the kennel, in a large open meadow along a creek bottom called the Whiteface Intervale. The meadow had no established trails, so Armstrong used a whip to train the dogs to follow directional commands. He would crack the twenty-five-foot whip along the left side of the team and tell the dogs to "gee over." They were forced to move to the right to get away from the whip crack. Cracking the whip on the right with the command "haw over" made them move to the left. With practice he could move the team over as far as he wanted, and soon the dogs followed verbal commands alone. A whip was used on dogs only as needed for discipline.[14]

Soldiers from Fort Pepperel, Maine, came to Chinook Kennels in January 1943 for a publicity performance. Troops lashed .30-caliber machine guns to the sleds. With a gunner and an assistant gunner wearing white parkas for camouflage, teams were paraded around so newspaper and newsreel photographers could take promotional pictures. The gun crews unhooked their teams from the sleds, donned gas masks, and theatrically pushed the sleds through smoke produced by smoke grenades. They also fired live ammunition across the Intervale into a hill for the photographers' benefit.[15] The entire operation was strictly for propaganda and public relations,[16] and photographs were published in various periodicals. The notoriety engen-

FIGURE 2.4. Wonalancet sled mounted with .30-caliber water-cooled machine gun at Chinook Kennels in January 1943. (Courtesy of Lynne Mace)

dered good public exposure for Chinook Kennels, the army, and the Dogs for Defense program.

Machine guns were never again mounted on dogsleds. This technique might have been used if the planned invasion of Norway had happened, since dog teams had been envisioned working with the First Special Service Force in commando operations.[17] But all subsequent versions of dog transportation field manuals included machine guns and their ammunition as typical freight for combat loads carried by dog teams.

Shortly after the publicity exploits in January 1943, the entire Chinook Kennels contingent was shipped to Camp Rimini, recently established in Montana. Forty dogs in their shipping crates, harnesses, sleds, and dog food were loaded aboard a single railroad car with Dick Moulton, Dave Armstrong, and Bob Brown along to supervise. The train made its way slowly across the country by way of Boston and Chicago. Dogs were allowed to run loose in the car for exercise during the trip. Finally they were off-loaded at Helena, Montana, and put onto trucks that arrived at Camp Rimini on February 3, 1943.[18]

Chinook Kennels was tapped by military authorities at the inception of the

FIGURE 2.5. Cpl. Danny Feurborn (*standing*) looks on while Pvt. Donald V. Anderson removes a husky from a shipping crate. Dogs were shipped by railroad cars from Chinook Kennels to Camp Rimini in January 1943. (U.S. Army Military History Institute)

sled dog program. Because he was a civilian, Milton Seeley managed to avoid much of the red tape that encumbered the military bureaucracy. He was able to get military personnel transferred to the fledgling program promptly and to obtain the necessary equipment and supplies. But Seeley's official business with the army terminated shortly after the dogs and men arrived at Rimini. He did make one personal inspection tour of the sled dog facility at the camp to ensure that adequate equipment was available for training dogs and operating the kennels. Seeley died shortly after he returned home to New Hampshire. [19] Chinook Kennels' association with the military was a brief episode, but the expertise and influence generated by its former employees guided the entire military sled dog program throughout the war. Supplying sled dogs for all of Byrd's expeditions established Chinook Kennels as the United States' most authoritative and knowledgeable resource center.

3. Sled Dogs and Ski Troops

Camp Hale, Colorado

The most unusual U.S. military unit of World War II was the Tenth Mountain Division. It was formed at Fort Lewis, Washington, in December 1941, then established at Camp Hale, Colorado, in 1942. The unit comprised skiers, climbers, cowboys, mule skinners, and other outdoorsmen including dogsled drivers. The Tenth was initially under the provisional command of the Mountain Training Center, whose responsibilities included training, developing equipment, and originating doctrine for the mountain unit. The foundation mission of this distinctive tactical unit was the invasion of Norway. The concept was that dog teams could resupply fighting forces moving cross country, so they were extensively analyzed and experimented with from the earliest development of the mountain division.

The K-9 Detachment was commanded by 2nd Lt. Stuart A. Mace, a former climber and botanist who had absolutely no experience with dog teams. His only knowledge of sled dogs was from stories told by an uncle who had been an exploratory mining engineer in Alaska. While serving with a combat engineer company in the newly formed mountain unit, Mace was ordered to the commander's office and told that he was "in the dog house now." Mace had been uneasy about his audience with his superior, since he was a conscientious objector. He had completely forgotten volunteering for the job as K-9 commander. He was relieved to hear about his new assignment, which he believed would be a perfect opportunity to serve his country without taking up arms against other human beings. Mace learned that the mission of the K-9 Detachment was fourfold: sled dogs, messenger dogs, attack dogs, and pack dogs. But the sled dog venture had the highest priority. As he described it, "the entire operation was a four ring circus." [1]

This detachment included former dog drivers from Alaska, New England,

FIGURE 3.1. Sled dog team and Tenth Mountain Division ski troops at Cooper Hill, winter 1943–44. Cooper Hill was the ski training area near Camp Hale. The Sled is the Wonalancet type. (Photo by Ralph Ball. Denver Public Library, Western History Collection, F-44581)

and Byrd's Antarctic expeditions. Their disparate experiences meant that they took significantly different approaches during the entire developmental period of dogsled doctrine. The ideas of the "Alaskan" contingent were based on the opinions of people like Neil C. Curtis and Carl Wheeler, both former dogsled freighters. [2] Although Wheeler was from the Mesabi Iron Range in northeastern Minnesota, not from Alaska, his experiences reflected the Alaskan style of mushing while carrying heavy freight. He had been drafted along with his entire dog team and sent to Camp Hale. [3] These men were used to deeper and softer snow. Their approach was actually closer to military needs in a high mountain environment than that of those who had polar experience. [4] Ed Moody belonged to the polar faction—drivers who were more used to hard, icy conditions. The New England set were all former racers, used to light sleds and fast dogs. [5] As a result, ideas about sled construction and dog handling differed markedly between the factions. Having no experience with dogs, Mace was able to step back from heated opinions and glean the best from all the approaches. [6]

One problem that quickly became apparent during training, which was also a problem at Camp Rimini, was the use of personal dog teams. Although dog teams usually did work best for particular drivers, this practice was not ideal for military operations, since drivers would frequently be required to drive someone else's team. Mace was taught this lesson early in his sled dog experience at Camp Hale. Mace drove Carl Wheeler's team to the train station at Pando (down the road from Camp Hale) to meet his mother and wife. While he was returning with the women on a sled, a "weasel" (an experimental over-snow vehicle similar to a modern snowcat) pulled out in front of the team from a side street. Wheeler's startled dogs did not respond to Mace's commands, and the team piled up in a huge accordion-style wreck and started an enormous dogfight in the middle of the street.[7]

The opinions of experienced dog drivers of lesser rank were often over-ruled by senior officers with little experience, sometimes with unfortunate consequences.[8] One such officer was a Frenchman who had written a book about his experiences living in the Canadian bush. He had been given a direct commission into the U.S. Army and was sent to Camp Hale because of his "expertise." He added little to the sled dog program and even opposed building workable sleds. His opinion was that all dog freighting should use toboggans. Unfortunately, his opinion carried considerable weight with the Mountain and Winter Warfare Board, which directed the sled dog program. It was not until that person was finally moved out of his position that strides were made in sled development.[9]

Every available piece of equipment for dogsledding was tested at Camp Hale, including harnesses, hitches, sleds, and toboggans.[10] A standard was established for numbers of dogs and types of equipment, which became the basis of army field manual FM 25-6, *Dog Transportation*, dated 1944.

Camp Hale's K-9 Detachment tested various sleds and toboggans meant for use in support of every field operation by mountain infantry regiments, driving them all over the area's mountain ranges.[11] In addition, dog teams from Wonalancet, New Hampshire, and Rimini, Montana, visited for several months to conduct supplementary testing.[12] The teams they trained were used to resupply troops and evacuate those injured on maneuvers to roadheads. On one field training exercise musher Vernon Gardner was driving a team when he encountered Brig. Gen. O. S. Rolfe (president of the Mountain and Winter Warfare Board) along the trail. When General Rolfe reached out to pat the dogs, Gardner bellowed at him not to pet his dogs

FIGURE 3.2. In deep snow, men on snowshoes had to break trail for dog teams.
Dog teams supported every field exercise conducted by the fledgling
Tenth Mountain Division. (Courtesy of Lynne Mace)

when they were working. General Rolfe stopped in his tracks, incredulous
at such effrontery from an enlisted man. Gardner's lead dog was a malamute
named Silver, who immediately urinated on the general's boots, adding
further insult. To mark the occasion, some other drivers later photographed
Silver wearing a miniature ski cap with a star cut out of tinfoil.[13]

The K-9 area was next to the division's mule barns, which caused more
than one interesting interchange. K-9 staff watched with great amusement as
mule skinners tried to put snowshoes on the mules.[14] The mule pack artillery
commander, Col. David Rufner, had offered a two-grade advancement for
anyone who could develop a mule snowshoe. "This would be quite a feat,"
the dog drivers were quick to point out, "since army mules could not even
get to maneuver areas during the winter."[15] There was great competition
between mule skinners and dog drivers over which animals were the best
freight carriers. On one occasion a dog team was driven to the top of
Homestake Peak (over 13,000 feet high) just to prove to the mule skinners
that it could be done.[16]

Equipment was evaluated and reports were forwarded to the Department

FIGURE 3.3. Modified convertible sled-toboggan with five-dog tandem hitch being tested in the mountains above Camp Hale. The lead dog is Silver, who urinated on Brig. Gen. O. S. Rolfe's boots. Photo by Winston Pote. (Courtesy of Lynne Mace)

of the Army. The K-9 crew discovered what polar explorers had found many years before—that sleds and sledges were easier to pull than toboggans, particularly on hard pack or in icy conditions.[17] Toboggans could not carry as heavy loads, either, because they had a larger area of surface contact. Early on in equipment trials it had been determined that the sledges and toboggans currently available were totally unsuited to the deep snow conditions found in the Rocky Mountains. Men on snowshoes had to walk ahead and pack trails, then let the snow harden overnight before dog teams could travel, a common technique in Alaskan freighting operations. Sled teams supporting ski troops arrived before them and had a comfortable camp established by the time the skiers got there. Yet division staff objected because sled dog drivers used snowshoes instead of skis.[18]

From all the information generated by Camp Hale testers, Headquarters, Service and Supply in Washington DC rendered the opinion that "the development of a dog sledge was not of sufficient importance to warrant an in depth development project, since the need for them was limited, and that sufficient quantities of sleds were available from commercial suppliers in Canada, Alaska, and the northern United States." [19] After the invasion of Norway was canceled, it was officially stated that no one contemplated any dog team use for supply of a mountain division. There were simply not enough dogs available for the task. Moreover, when conditions were suitable for use of dogs, over-snow vehicles such as the newly developed weasel could be used instead. [20]

In March 1943 General Rolfe requested that a dogsled be constructed locally with funds allotted by the board. He wanted it compared with a modified convertible sled-toboggan to determine which was best suited for the mountain terrain. [21] The dog drivers themselves favored this request, since they were unhappy with all of the current sled designs, particularly the convertible sled-toboggan, which the upper echelon favored because of its low cost, availability, and attempted standardization. [22] The sled-toboggan was made of laminated maple and was originally designed as a man-hauled sled. As built, its runners were so short that a driver could not even stand on them. The stanchions that supported the bed off the runners were so wide that snow built up between them, causing extreme drag. Since the sled was only twenty inches wide it was very unstable, and keeping it upright was immeasurably difficult. Dog drivers hated this sled so much that they symbolically burned one. [23] The drivers eventually modified the original version to make it more favorable for use with dogs, extending the runners by five inches and adding a brush bow (essentially a bumper on the front of the sled to prevent damage from trees, rocks, brush, etc.), a foot-operated brake, and keels or "slew brakes" down the center of the runners. With these modifications the convertible sled-toboggan proved to be much more utilitarian, [24] but the design changes were never approved for general use.

Authorization for a locally produced sled was finally granted. The "all purpose dog sled," which became known also as the "army standard mountain sled," was designed with the help of Ed Moody, an experienced sled builder from New England. Moody was also a dog racer and had served as a dog handler on Byrd's second Antarctic expedition in 1933. The many innovations attempting to overcome the shortcomings of all the sleds tested so far produced a basket sled ten feet long. The major problem with earlier sleds was that they could not float on top of the deep powder snow encountered in the Rocky Mountains. The newly designed sled was equipped with skilike runners four and a half inches wide with steel edges, which helped keep the sled from sliding downslope when contouring on steep hills. Its runners also had "keels" running their entire length to prevent sideslipping, as well as slew brakes. On hardpack the sled rode on the keels, with less surface in contact with the snow and therefore less drag. [25] Ed Moody produced only one such sled, at the Groswald Ski Company in Denver, one of the manufacturers of skis for the Tenth Mountain Division. This sled received limited testing in the spring of 1943, just before the K-9 Detachment was transferred to Camp Rimini, Montana. [26] In spite of its limited testing, it was considered far superior in all respects to every sled previously tested, including the convertible sled-toboggan that had been modified for dog team use. [27] Moody's sled later became known as the Camp Hale sled. It was the basis for all future sleds built and used by the U.S. Army.

The romance associated with dog teams became a thing of the past as the Tenth Mountain Division prepared for its new assignment in Europe after the planned invasion of Norway was canceled. A dog unit table of organization and equipment was devised and submitted for the Tenth Division, but it was never approved. [28] On June 16, 1943, the entire K-9 Detachment was shipped to Camp Rimini, near Helena, Montana, to augment the Sled Dog Center. Dog teams and equipment were tested and used at Camp Hale for only one winter. Although it was generally demonstrated that dogs alone could not resupply an entire infantry division, [29] dog teams supporting the Tenth Mountain Division certainly proved their worth in other specialized tasks such as casualty evacuation. [30] Tough lessons learned in the mountains around Camp Hale, Colorado, laid the framework for all future doctrine. It was here that fundamental tenets were established, paving the way for later missions using dogs for search and rescue in polar regions.

4. Sled Dog Center

Camp Rimini, Montana

The central focus for all sled dog doctrine, training, and sled building during World War II was Camp Rimini, Montana. Here the most significant advances in military dogsledding were nurtured, including refinement of the dogs themselves through a breeding program, improved training techniques, and organizational equipment assigned to military units.

Camp Rimini was established as part of the Dogs for Defense program in which civilians donated dogs to be used in the war effort, with the promise that they would be returned to their owners after the war. More than twenty thousand were donated for duty as messenger dogs, sentry dogs, attack dogs, sled dogs, and pack dogs. Camp Rimini became the War Dog Reception and Training Center for all sled dogs and pack dogs.[1] Few sled dogs were donated because malamutes and Siberian huskies were not prominent breeds in the United States at this time, so the government bought most of them from owners in Alaska and Canada. Dogs were then shipped to Camp Rimini for training. It was originally thought that dogs would be used for the invasion of Norway. Later their primary mission became search and rescue in Arctic and subarctic areas.

In September 1942 the Department of Agriculture authorized the U.S. Army Quartermaster Corps to use Civilian Conservation Corps Camp F-79, thirteen miles from Helena, Montana.[2] Thus Camp Rimini was born. The camp itself was near an old silver mining town named Rimini, just at the base of the Continental Divide in the Rocky Mountains. The area provided much snow and cold weather for sled dog operations. It also had plenty of training space, with multiple trails running through adjacent national forests. Since the site included both heavy timber and open terrain, the camp was ideal for training dog teams headed to Alaska and the Arctic.[3]

FIGURE 4.1. Dog kennel area at Camp Rimini. (Courtesy of Greg Stevens)

The original commanding officer of Camp Rimini was a Quartermaster remount officer, Maj. E. J. Purfield. Major Purfield's previous duty assignment had been overseeing the breeding of horses obtained from ranchers, using fine bloodstock provided by the military to produce high-quality horses for the army. Purfield had no experience with dogs of any kind, let alone sled dogs, but he was intelligent enough to let his few experienced subordinates run the operation without interference while he primarily directed the overall military functions of the camp.[4]

Second in command (the camp administrative officer) was a reserve officer, Capt. Lawrence C. Phipps Jr., who was well known for running his pack of foxhounds in Colorado Springs, Colorado.[5] But like Purfield, Phipps had no expertise with sled dogs.

The only commissioned expert there at the beginning was 1st Lt. James J. Patnode, who came from Lake Placid, New York, where he and his brothers had raced dog teams in the wooded upstate area. Patnode had been directly commissioned into the army as an expert and was the only officer of the group originally assigned who had any kind of experience with sled dogs.[6]

The person most influential in actually training dogs and drivers at Camp

Rimini was M.Sgt. Richard S. Moulton of the Canine Section. Moulton had worked at Chinook Kennels in Wonalancet, New Hampshire, for several years. He had also been a dog driver for Admiral Byrd on his 1939 Antarctic expedition. After he returned from Antarctica, Moulton was drafted into the army and sent to Baffin Land.[7] Later he was reassigned to Camp Rimini. Moulton's extensive practical knowledge included preparing expedition equipment, running a large kennel, training and transporting dogs, and driving teams in situations other than racing. From the beginning he was considered the primary expert, and he kept this position throughout the existence of Camp Rimini, reporting directly to the commanding officer.[8] In spite of his prodigious responsibilities and knowledge, Moulton remained a noncommissioned officer for the duration of World War II.

Another former employee from Chinook Kennels who was sent to Camp Rimini was David W. Armstrong Jr. Armstrong had also worked at Chinook Kennels for several summers and had been identified to the army by Milton J. Seeley (the owner of the kennels) as having extensive knowledge about sled dogs. After a short stint in basic training, Armstrong accompanied Moulton to Camp Rimini in February 1943. They brought forty dogs, several sleds, harnesses, and bags of dog food across the United States in a railroad car. When they arrived at Camp Rimini, the men found few people and very few dogs. Their string of forty dogs considerably increased the overall dog population at the camp.[9]

Men and dogs continued to arrive at the camp every day, including almost anyone with any previous competence with sled dogs. Dog drivers came from all over the country—New England, New York, Idaho, Minnesota, and Alaska. Like the assemblage at Camp Hale, they all brought with them regional differences in their approaches to dogsledding.[10]

Eddie Barbeau, of French Canadian and Ojibwa ancestry, arrived from Leech Lake Reservation in northern Minnesota bringing seventeen sled dogs and his wife. Eddie's dogs had been used to haul supplies for the U.S. Fish and Game Department while checking on trapline operations in the North Country. These dogs had also hauled freight for the International Boundary Commission during surveys along the Canadian border. Barbeau had made his living from sled dogs his entire life, doing not only freighting but racing and carnival performances as well. He had also served as a purchasing agent buying sled dogs for the government before he was recruited by the military. Barbeau was considered an excellent dog trainer and could train dogs others deemed unsuitable.[11] One dog had been purchased as a good lead dog, but no one could get it to do anything. It was considered worthless, yet it took Barbeau just minutes to have the dog working perfectly. The secret was that this dog, purchased in Canada, had been trained in French. Barbeau simply gave the dog commands in its "native" tongue. Eddie's wife Kay, who was a dog musher herself, ran the local USO.[12]

Other mushers also brought their own dog teams, as did Leon La Fave from Tupper Lake, New York. Like Barbeau, La Fave was of French Canadian descent. His commands were given with a French Canadian nasal sound that no one else could duplicate, so he was the only person who could drive his team. He would often bet other soldier drivers fifty dollars that they would not be able to drive his team from one end of camp to the other. He always won. They could not even get his dogs on their feet. La Fave was ultimately sent "north" with his team (to active duty with a search and rescue unit), since he was the only one who could use them.

When 2nd Lt. Stuart A. Mace came to Camp Rimini in April 1943, he brought all the experience he had gained at Camp Hale. He was put in charge of developing a pack dog program. Pack dogs were meant to be used by search and rescue units during snowless periods in subarctic areas. No one who had ever been a dog driver or associated with sled dogs wanted to work with pack dogs, so the pack dog contingent was developed from nonmushers.[13] Mace's area of expertise expanded to include Alaska and western Canada, where he was sent on inspection tours of search and rescue detachments. As the supply of sled dogs diminished, he also went there to buy dogs. In addition to his other responsibilities, Mace worked on a scheme for parachuting sled dogs. He built a test tower for dropping dogs from two large pine trees. After practicing with this technique, he did live dog drops from aircraft.[14]

The training of men and dogs at Camp Rimini varied according to their experience. At first, most men reached the camp generally skilled in dog driving and only had to be trained in winter survival skills. Since the whole sled dog program was still evolving, the early arrivals' way of doing things fundamentally became "the army way." Overall training was geared to using the sled loads that teams would encounter on a typical mission. There were some problems with drivers from racing circuits, however: many racers were known to get out of sight of the main camp, unload their sleds, and race around carrying no loads. Although that was certainly great fun for all, it did not do much toward conditioning dogs to haul heavy loads or training drivers to handle heavily loaded sleds. Another problem was race drivers' "whip and whistle" driving. Many of them had used a small whip to signal their dogs, and others used a shrill whistle to encourage dogs to run faster. Like personal dog teams and French Canadian accents, whip and whistle driving did not match the military tenet that all teams should be able to perform for all drivers.[15] It was generally thought that most dogs could be retrained more easily than many of the "more experienced" drivers.[16] The time available for training new recruits was extremely variable. If filler teams and drivers were needed for the rescue units, their training might be only six weeks long. At other times with no pressure, training might last as long as three months.[17]

Initially new drivers were matched up with experienced drivers. At first they both rode together on the sled runners so the novices could learn driving basics, then new drivers were given a fully trained team to run alone. Training culminated in a trail test conducted by Sergeant Moulton. The problems he identified were discussed with the new drivers, and they were given some time to practice the correct techniques. Then they were checked out again on the trail. A major problem was that new drivers tended to make pets of their favorite dogs. They would bring the dogs into the barracks and play with them, undermining the discipline needed in a working dog.[18]

John Eslick, a trainer at Camp Rimini, had a standard orientation spiel: "A dog is not just a dumb animal. You need to be much smarter than the dog to be a dog driver. Few men are smarter than these dogs." Army doctrine stated that experienced drivers should use whips only to break up dogfights. Many new drivers were inclined to believe they should crack the whip to make the dogs run harder, in the romantic Hollywood image of a dog musher. Eslick would provide his own team for a new recruit's first overnight run. Eslick would warn the soldier driver not to use a whip, since his dogs would not respond to it. As soon as the team was out of sight, a new driver would give in to the temptation and crack his whip over the team. Immediately the team would do a 180-degree turn, spilling the sled contents and the driver along the trail. Then the dogs would race back to the main camp, where Eslick would be waiting. When the trainee finally caught up with the team, Eslick would dress him down and he would then have to drive the team back to recover the sled load scattered all along the trail and then catch up to the rest of his group.[19]

FIGURE 4.2. The cold weather and rugged terrain of Camp Rimini provided the primary training for Arctic survival that was not taught in formal classes. (Courtesy of John A. Matovich)

No formal structure for Arctic and cold weather indoctrination was feasible because of the varied skill levels of the troops to be trained and the camp's limited resources. Many phases of instruction were imparted through hearing about the experiences of other drivers in "bull sessions." Arctic survival training and winter camping techniques were not taught in formal classes but were learned by simply spending time on the trail. The primary survival instructors were the cold weather and rugged terrain of Camp Rimini.[20]

In most cases an experienced driver was given three complete teams to train, rotating them in harness. The conclusive test of a team's training was its being driven by another driver. One of the biggest problems in training dog teams was having all drivers give verbal commands in close to the same intonation or timbre. In the final shakedown of a team, another driver would confirm that a team would respond to his commands, ensuring that the dogs could be handled by someone else. After the teams were shipped off to various units, however, most drivers in the "North" drove only two alternating teams, since dogs ultimately worked best for a single driver they became used to. Most dogs were trainable, but some older dogs and dogs with highly independent personalities would not adapt to "the army way."[21]

During months when snow was not available at lower elevations, drivers exercised dogs by the same technique that had been used at Chinook Kennels. They hitched teams up to old automobile chassis and drove them to the snow line above Camp Rimini. There the dogs would be changed over to sleds, and training would continue around Red Mountain at the Gould Diggings area. During July and August, teams were not usually run.[22]

Dogs were used for as many tasks as possible to maximize their training time. When log cabins were built as dog harness rooms, teams were used to snake logs out of the forest above camp.[23] Dog teams were also used to haul elk that drivers killed during hunting season. On one occasion a team of fifteen dogs was hitched to an elk with a rope tied around the base of its antlers. Two men walked alongside holding the tips of the antlers, and the team easily pulled the big bull through timber and deadfall. The elk measured forty-eight and a half inches between its antler tips and was estimated to weigh over eight hundred pounds. All the elk that were shot supplemented military rations.[24]

Besides training dogs and drivers, the staff at Camp Rimini also procured sled dogs for the army. They traveled to Canada and Alaska, buying one or two dogs at a time from local trappers. Dogs were then collected and shipped back to Camp Rimini. Because dog teams were so essential to indigenous populations, they could buy only a few dogs in any one area. In some instances they even bartered glass beads for Indian dogs.[25] On one such buying trip, Sergeant Moulton purchased fifty-four sled dogs that Dave Armstrong had to take back to Camp Rimini by rail. Sergeant Armstrong and the dogs traversed Canada in a baggage car with few problems. After they arrived in Helena, only one dog required medical attention because of fighting with others.[26] Lieutenant Mace also went on buying trips. He remarked, "During that period, local Mounted Police were the equivalent of the Northern Mafia. Nothing purchased from the natives was allowed out of the area without a percentage being paid to them. Without their cooperation, nothing could be accomplished."[27]

FIGURE 4.3. As dogs from New England and Alaska became scarce, the military sought dogs from everywhere. These are Greenland dogs in military harness. (Courtesy of Lynne Mace)

Before long it became clear that it was getting extremely difficult to obtain sled dogs. Most of the stock in New England had been used up, and the supply from Canada was drying up as well. Since no one knew how long the war would continue, a breeding program for sled dogs was started at Camp Rimini. Dogs that came from good stock in Canada or the United States and were not issued to active rescue units were held back to begin this program. The army's attempt to breed sled dogs with Arctic wolves also had its inception at Camp Rimini during this time. Breeding projects were only beginning when Camp Rimini was closed down.[28]

The veterinary officer assigned to Camp Rimini was Capt. Sydney M. Smith, who treated both dogs and men until a physician was assigned, since the nearest military medical facility was in Helena, about thirteen miles away. The army built and equipped an excellent animal clinic at Camp Rimini. Captain Smith's innovative efforts kept all the dogs healthy during their tenure at the camp. Tapeworms were a serious problem in all dogs purchased in Canada that had been fed frozen freshwater fish. David Armstrong stated, "It was not a pretty sight driving a dog team down the

FIGURE 4.4. Some of the varied sled designs built at the Camp Rimini sled shop. (Courtesy of John A. Matovich)

road with tapeworms several feet long hanging out behind the dogs." Many dogs purchased in the Canadian Arctic suffered from a resistant strain of worms even after treatment. "Kidney worms" grew up to ten inches long, destroying the kidneys and finally killing the dogs. Captain Smith developed a surgical procedure for removing kidney worms and then flushing the kidney with a saline solution, allowing dogs to return to duty.[29]

One large Canadian dog did not seem to benefit from Captain Smith's ministrations. He grew skinnier every day and did not pass as many worms as other dogs after worming. One day he was seen twisting and hacking in great distress until finally he coughed up an object about a foot long. It turned out to be an Indian's moosehide jacket, complete with decorative beadwork. The dog had swallowed it, almost completely blocking his digestive tract. After regurgitating it, the dog prospered. The standing joke became, "I wonder when he's going to cough up the Indian."[30]

Eventually soldiers manufactured everything needed for dog team operations right at the camp. Except for sleds purchased early in the war, every sled used by the U.S. Army was designed, tested, or built at Camp Rimini. The sled shop used steam equipment to bend the hardwoods required for sleds. Originally a civilian named James Fritz was in charge. He claimed to have built sleds at one time, but most people considered him a detriment to the entire sled building venture. It was said that he could "Fritz up" any good idea.[31] When sled builder Ed Moody came to Camp Rimini from the K-9 Detachment at Camp Hale, he strongly influenced design and building techniques.[32]

One person who did valuable work at the sled shop was Sgt. John A. Matovich. It was through his own hard work (primarily trial and error plus native skill) that he became the sled construction expert, since he had no experience in building dogsleds. His craftsmanship was evident in every sled that was built at Camp Rimini.[33] Matovich commented, "We were always trying to build a better mousetrap,"[34] so each sled that was built was improved in quality and design.

Most dog drivers did a rotation in the sled shop so they could learn sled construction firsthand. Sleds were their lifeline when they went to their final assignments in the Arctic, and drivers needed to know how to repair them when they were damaged.[35]

Technician 5th Class Edwin A. Dungan was the only person assigned to the canvas shop. He had run a harness and saddle shop in Cody, Wyoming, and single-handedly made all the dog harnesses and dog packs.[36] Dungan helped develop and manufacture the dog parachute harnesses that were tested at Camp Rimini.

There were never more than 150 men in total at Camp Rimini. Most were part of the workforce necessary for a military organization to function: cooks, truck drivers, carpenters, medics, butchers, veterinary assistants, and headquarters staff. At any one time the camp never had more than fifty trainers, dog drivers, pack dog handlers, and trainees. There is no record of the number of dogs at Camp Rimini, but it is believed to have been between eight hundred and a thousand, including all sled dogs and pack dogs.[37]

Camp Rimini was ordered closed in March 1944 because the army could not justify operating a separate facility just for sled and pack dogs. All canine operations across the country were consolidated at Fort Robinson, Nebraska, and Front Royal, Virginia. After operating for less than two years at Camp Rimini, the entire sled dog and pack dog enterprise was transported by rail to Fort Robinson, Nebraska. At this same time, many dog drivers and teams were shipped off to search and rescue units across the Arctic and eastern Canada to fill operational quotas. Only about 225 sled dogs and 25 pack dogs ended up being relocated to Fort Robinson. [38] This ended the most significant era in the remarkably short history of sled dog operations in the U.S. Army during World War II.

5. Sled Dog Deactivation

Fort Robinson, Nebraska

In the spring of 1944, as the Allied forces were staging for the invasion of Fortress Europe, Camp Rimini was deactivated, and all its canine activities were moved to Fort Robinson, Nebraska. In an effort to consolidate diverse operations across the country that were sapping limited support manpower, the army closed canine centers at Front Royal, Virginia, San Carlos, California, and Camp Rimini, Montana. Relocating all dog activities to a more central locale alleviated considerable duplication of effort, particularly in administration and supply.[1]

Because of its practical experience in handling animals as a Quartermaster remount depot, Fort Robinson was established as a War Dog Reception and Training Center in 1942. Before the sled dog and pack dog training program was relocated from Camp Rimini, K-9 Detachment staff at Fort Robinson had trained dogs for guard duty, attack duty, scouting, and messenger use. When the post was initially established as a canine facility, a state-of-the-art eighty-kennel dog veterinary hospital was built and staffed.[2] Thousands of horses were also quartered at Fort Robinson. Many of these had been condemned, ready for slaughter. This steady supply of dog food was another logistical reason for consolidation here. Dogs would eat well.

After moving to Fort Robinson the sled dog program was reestablished on a 10,000-acre wooded reserve at another 1930s Civilian Conservation Corps camp. As at Camp Rimini, dogs at Fort Robinson were kenneled on a river bottom surrounded by buttes. But here there were fewer dogs and fewer people. In anticipation of Camp Rimini's deactivation, many drivers and teams had been assigned to various search and rescue squadrons. At the same time, many dogs that were not progressing as hoped were disposed of and not shipped to Fort Robinson. It was a monumental task to

FIGURE 5.1. Dog training continued after the move to Fort Robinson, using proven techniques. Here another "Cream Team" undergoes warm-weather training. (Courtesy of Lynne Mace)

dispatch sled dogs, pack dogs, sled building equipment, the harness shop, and other ongoing projects to a new location over six hundred miles away and reestablish them there.[3]

Four key individuals executed the move from Camp Rimini: 2nd Lt. Stuart A. Mace, head of the pack dog section; M.Sgt. Richard S. Moulton, in charge of training all drivers and dogs; Sgt. John A. Matovich, from the sled shop; and Technician 5th Class Edwin A. Dungan from the harness shop. Lt. James J. Patnode, head of the sled dog section, did not make the move to Fort Robinson because he had just been court-martialed. Patenode had illegally arranged for one of his dogs to be sold to his wife as surplus for $7.50. This dog was then sold to Pfc. Malcolm G. Douglass for $300.[4] The dog, Lucky, had been part of the U.S. Antarctic expedition in 1939–41. Douglass had also served on this expedition, where he grew attached to Lucky. Shortly after he was born in the Antarctic, the dog had fallen down a crevasse, breaking both forelegs. Not long afterward he almost burned to death in a blubber-house fire. After surviving the fire, he was christened Lucky.[5] Douglass ended up with Lucky, and Lieutenant Patnode was dismissed from the service.

FIGURE 5.2. One of the projects that continued after the move from Camp Rimini to Fort Robinson was the building and testing of "Big Bertha" for the First Arctic Search and Rescue Squadron in Greenland. The ax-handle stanchion sled is shown being tested on the 10,000-acre wooded reserve. (Courtesy of Lynne Mace)

Two sled projects that had been started at Camp Rimini and not completed until after the move to Fort Robinson were the Bagby-Johnson sled for use in Alaska and the "Big Bertha" sled for use by the First Arctic Search and Rescue Squadron in Greenland. The Bagby-Johnson sled had been designed at Camp Rimini, and a prototype had been built. But a dozen more sleds were needed in Alaska. These were built at Fort Robinson. "Big Bertha," built with stanchions made from ax handles, was not completed until after relocation to Fort Robinson. As soon as the Bagby—Johnson sleds were built they were sent to the navy survey project at the Petroleum Reserves in northern Alaska. The navy was providing only officers for this project, so all dogs, equipment, and drivers had to accompany the sleds on their voyage north. This operation totally stripped the sled dog program at Fort Robinson.[6]

Manpower was fortunately available for many housekeeping requirements of the post: German prisoners of war. Beginning in March 1943, POWs were housed at Fort Robinson. Having POWs perform maintenance functions allowed the few remaining dog people to concentrate on dog-related tasks.

One endeavor that used POWs was the sled shop. Many of the POWs who worked there were skilled carpenters and woodworkers from the German navy. These men knew nothing about dogsleds, but under the close supervision of Sergeant Matovich, their excellent skills were fully utilized. That there were no civilian "experts" in the chain of command allowed a tighter rein on operations, so the entire program ran more smoothly.[7] The prisoners enjoyed their work because it occupied their time and they earned eighty cents a day.[8]

Just before the end of the war, Sergeant Matovich built models of all the sleds that the sled shop had designed and built during the war. These miniature replicas were true to their full-size counterparts in every detail. The models were sent to the War Department to illustrate the creativity, innovation, and overall enterprise of the sled shop. None are known to exist today. Many people assume they were filched as souvenirs.[9] Photographs were also taken of all the sleds for a report, but it was never completed.

Considerable attempts were made to standardize various sled designs at Fort Robinson, primarily because there were few "individualists" working in the sled shop who wanted customized equipment. The German prisoners simply did what they were told.

A primary sled dog project that started coming to fruition during the time at Fort Robinson was the experiment with breeding dogs with Arctic wolves. Many people in the sled dog program recognized the potential in producing dogs with many wolf characteristics, primarily their huge size and "buoyant" feet. Siberian and Eskimo dogs had what was considered a high "ice foot," more appropriate for running on hardpack than in the deep snow that army mushers encountered in many places. Here at Fort Robinson, the breeding program attempted to cross the huge snowshoe foot and long legs of the Arctic wolf with the traits of heavy stock dogs. A half-wolf and half-malamute named Nikolai had been purchased in Alaska before the move to Fort Robinson. Nikolai was just beginning to produce wolf hybrids when the war started winding down. Project staff were told to continue with the experiment, since it was still necessary to resupply rescue units with dogs. The army never used Nikolai's pups, however, and breeding of sled dogs was officially discontinued in July 1945 by directive of the Quartermaster General. This untimely demise of the army's attempt to produce the ultimate freighting sled dog was a tragedy. The same directive that discontinued breeding stated that the total number of sled dogs and pack dogs on hand had to be reduced to ninety as soon as possible: the deadline was September 30, 1945.[10] The sled and pack dog program continued for another year after the war, directed by Sgt. Howard M. Travis. In June 1946 the whole program was totally deactivated. All the remaining dogs and most of the equipment on hand at this time were simply sold as surplus.[11]

The army sled dog program died at Fort Robinson with the end of World War II. Associated components that had been started at Camp Rimini died with it, including sled building, harness making, parachuting, pack dogs, team and musher training, and the wolf breeding experiment. Although sled dogs and pack dogs were still used by the U.S. Air Force for another ten years, there was never any attempt to maintain the expertise the army program had gained during the war. The sled dog program had been an army Quartermaster function, and by this time the air force had evolved into its own branch. Thus it was easy to see why the value of the sled dog program was overlooked, even though its primary purpose had always been search and rescue of downed aviators. The administrators believed that dogs, equipment, and expertise could easily be purchased as necessary from local civilian sources. The integral creativity and ingenuity generated by the sled dog program during the war was lost, buried by a modern U.S. military. All the highly trained dogs eventually disappeared into the snowy vistas of imagination—no longer needed by a progressive, streamlined war machine.

6. Soldiers' Sleds

U.S. Army Specifications

Unlike almost every other piece of equipment in the U.S. military inventory, army dogsleds were not standardized. For an organization that thrives on specifications and clonelike standards, dogsleds did not fit into the classic mold. Instead, they mirrored the individualists who drove them. Before the mass buildup of equipment and forces during World War II, sleds customarily used in remote areas of Alaska were locally produced. Every item of equipment authorized for use in any military organization was listed in the *Table of Organization and Equipment* (TOE). All TOE entries including those of the First Arctic Search and Rescue Squadron, the largest single user of dogsleds within the U.S. forces, listed sleds as a "nonstandard item." These unique items could not be procured through normal supply channels.

The early *FM 25–6, Basic Field Manual, Dog Team Transportation* (January 4, 1941) described four basic types of sleds and their specifications. However, these sleds were produced only in limited quantities by local woodworkers. The manual did serve as a guide for sleds that were later built under contract or by the army itself. Because sled specifications were only guidelines, soldiers in the field were granted much leeway for improvising equipment to best meet the unique situations they encountered.

The four sleds or sledges described in the early manual were a basket sled, a messenger sled, a toboggan, and a freight sled. The basket sled was a thirteen-foot cross-country sled made of hickory with six bays, weighing about 120 pounds. A bay was the area between the uprights, or stanchions. The sled was actually fourteen feet, four inches long, with a thirteen-foot cargo bed. It was twenty-two inches wide at the rear, tapering to twenty-one and three-quarters inches at the front. All joints were mortised and held together by rawhide lashings, or babiche. Cross lashings between stanchions were tightly

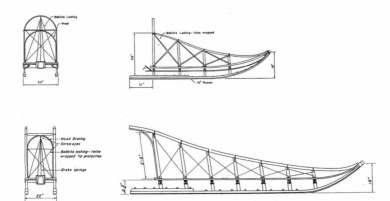

FIGURE 6.1. Messenger sled with eight- to nine-foot bed (*top*) compared with thirteen-foot freight sled (*bottom*) as shown in the 1941 version of *FM 25-6, Basic Field Manual, Dog Team Transportation*. Unlike the earlier-model freight sled illustrated in the 1926 technical regulation, this version gives the driver room to stand on the runners.

stretched babiche wrapped with number 3 cotton twine to discourage dogs from chewing on them. A bow, or nose, height that became standard was a minimum of eighteen inches, higher than most other basket sleds of that era.[1]

The messenger sled was built along the same lines as the thirteen-foot cross-country sled but had only an eight- or nine-foot bed, illustrating non-standard variations from the earliest beginnings of the specification process. This sled was twenty-two inches wide and was described as useful for fast travel with small loads. Both of these sleds had a brake mechanism consisting of steel prongs attached to a brake board brought back up by coil springs. Having the brake board attached at the front caused less strain on internal parts of the sled, and the long radius let the prongs meet the ground in a more parallel position, producing drag instead of a plowing effect.[2]

The toboggan was described as useful on deep, soft snow or where no trail had been broken. Its specifications called for a length of thirteen feet, six inches or "as desired," with a width of twenty-five inches. The bottom was flat, with no rocker effect. It did have low runners shod with metal to prevent sideslipping. Uprights, a top rail, and handlebars could be provided

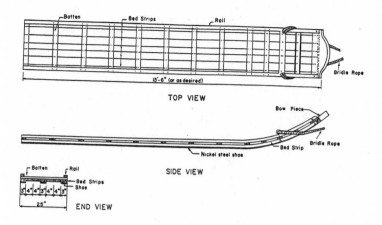

FIGURE 6.2. Sled-toboggan as illustrated in *FM 25-6, Basic Field Manual, Dog Team Transportation,* 1941.

"if desired." A chain brake (a loop of chain dragged under the bottom) was used to help slow the toboggan as needed.[3]

The freight sled was twelve to thirteen feet long and was designed primarily to move large, bulky items. It too was twenty-two inches wide but the nose was only fourteen inches high. It usually had no brake; dogs were to be unhitched from the sled and descent controlled by the driver riding a gee pole. (A wooden pole was attached to either front side of the sled to assist in directional control of a heavily loaded sled. Riding the pole entailed walking beside the sled and using the added leverage the pole provided to push or pull the front of the sled in the direction desired.) When small brakes were added (essentially a pivoting prong on the tail of each runner), a second person could apply them and help control the sled. On sidehills, the uphill brake could be used to keep the sled on course. These sleds were also intended to be linked together as trailers. A twelve-hundred-pound load would be divided, with six hundred pounds on the first sled, four hundred pounds on the first trailer, and the final two hundred pounds on the second trailer sled.[4]

The second version of the army field manual *FM 25-6, Dog Transportation,* published August 19, 1944, attempted to standardize sleds and sledges used

FIGURE 6.3. The Nansen sled, which had been used by polar explorers.
(Courtesy of Lynne Mace)

by the military. The attempt to standardize sled designs had its beginnings
with technical regulations as early as 1926. In this second version the term
sled was completely replaced by *sledge*. The field manual described equipment generally but omitted most details, recognizing the need for adaptation. By this time, most sled types had been tested and evaluated. Dogsled
operations as a whole had been determined not to be feasible for any large-
scale use. The sleds listed below are those that were most commonly used by
the military during World War II as described in the manual. I will discuss
their development and specifics in greater detail later.

The first sled described was the Nansen sled, a double-ended freight sled
that had been used by polar explorers throughout the Arctic and Antarctic.
It had been modified by adding a gee pole and attaching boards lengthwise
to the underside of the bridges, or cross members. These boards enabled the
sled to work like a toboggan in deep snow, but their primary function was
to keep the cross members from being damaged by sharp ice.[5] This sled was
a favorite of GIs for carrying and maneuvering large, bulky items such as fuel
or oil drums on Arctic airfields.

Another freight sled depicted was the Antarctic sled, a modified Nansen

FIGURE 6.4. Lightweight Antarctic sled. This thirteen-foot sled was built with the Czegka bridge arch for cross members, providing excellent capacity-to-weight ratio. It was a favorite sled to use as a trailer. (Courtesy of John A. Matovich)

type. It too was double-ended, but it was very light in construction. It used an arch design (called a Czegka bridge) for the cross members, allowing an extremely high capacity-to-weight ratio. Since the sled was originally designed for use on smooth snow and ice, it was recommended that steel shoes be added and that boards be lashed underneath the cross members as in the Nansen sled, for the same reasons. This sled and the Nansen type were the ones advocated for use as trailers.[6]

The basket sled portrayed was the most widely used of all types. It could be used for light freighting or as an ambulance in rescue operations. Mentioned were a version ten and a half feet long and a lighter nine-and-a-half foot version, or messenger sledge. The longer version weighed about 100 pounds. It could carry a normal 400-pound load, with a capacity load of 750 pounds.[7]

One illustration in the manual depicted a "Wonalancet" basket sled, but no specifications were listed. A convertible, collapsible basket sled constructed of plywood was also defined—a combination toboggan, freight sled, and basket sled. According to the manual, its normal load was 750 pounds and its capacity load was 1,200 pounds![8] In reality, the "sled-tobog-

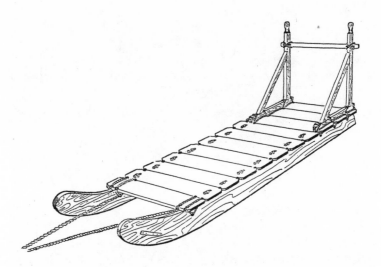

FIGURE 6.5. Native *komatik* sled as illustrated in the 1944 field manual, *FM 25-6, Dog Transportation.*

gan, convertible" was rated at a 400-pound capacity. The basket sled was considered easier to control, but it could not carry nearly the same load as a freight sled. Gee poles could be incorporated, but this sled was normally driven from the rear.

The native *komatik* or Greenland sledge was described as varying from six to thirty feet long and from fifteen to thirty inches wide. It was considered very satisfactory for general use, particularly with heavy loads over jagged sea ice. Considerable detail was written about the *komatik*, so that one could be built as required at "any northern army base if the terrain requires its use." The white people's version was to be constructed entirely of varnished ash. Runners were to be three-quarters of an inch thick and nine or ten inches high, shod with spring steel three-sixteenths of an inch thick by one and a quarter inches wide.[9]

The second version of the manual (1944) changed toboggan design. It recommended a length of at least nine feet, with a width of seventeen inches best for wooded areas. Seventeen inches conformed to the width of a snowshoe track, or the track of a dog team in single tandem. Twenty-two inches wide was considered better for ambulance work in open country.

The outside and center boards of the toboggan were to be thicker to prevent sideslipping. Army mushers objected to toboggans primarily because they could not carry as heavy a load as sleds owing to their larger friction surface. Additionally, loads carried through slush and water tended to get wet because there was zero ground clearance. [10]

The "Siwash" toboggan was explained as a native design seventeen inches wide and weighing thirty pounds. It was a three-board design held together by cleats. Handlebars were attached to the rear cleats, and ropes connected to the upturned front supported canvas sides. This toboggan was classified as excellent for ambulance work in wooded areas. [11] A letter from the Mountain and Winter Warfare Board at Camp Hale, Colorado, to the Army War College in Washington DC in March 1943 stated that "any anticipated dog team freighting would be with toboggans under conditions where over snow vehicles would not work." It also stated that "toboggans received thus far for testing were unsatisfactory" and that toboggans suitable for use with dogs had been ordered from Canada. This commercially obtained toboggan was similar to the three-board Siwash design.

The "Wonalancet" sled was originally designed and built by Arthur King, a woodworker who lived near Chinook Kennels in Wonalancet, New Hampshire. Chinook Kennels procured and trained scores of dogs for military sled teams during World War II. The Wonalancet sled was based on experience gained by teams in both the Antarctic and Alaska. It is the only true basket sled built by civilians and purchased in quantity by the military during that time. King originally built it in his basement, and later it was made by a furniture-manufacturing company in Pennsylvania. The Wonalancet sled is truly a combination toboggan and sled. Its dimensions and major design features were used as a model for the entire military program to develop a basket sled. This sled was eight feet long without the brush bow (bumper) and twenty-four inches wide overall. The width at the front was twenty-two inches on center, tapering to twenty-one inches at the rear, allowing for good tracking. It was thirty-one inches high and was built with five stanchions. A toboggan effect was achieved by attaching three six-inch boards under the crosspieces. The center board also served as the brake board, bolted only at the nose and at the second cross member. When the sled's narrow runners sank into soft snow, a load could theoretically float on its toboggan bottom. Runners were two inches wide and shod with cold rolled iron one-eighth of an inch thick, since spring steel was not available. The runners had a one-inch rocker, one-half inch forward and one-half inch rearward of the third stanchion. A foot-operated brake board had two steel prongs bolted to it to provide drag for stopping and was brought back up by coil springs. The Wonalancet sled was originally constructed of white ash coated with creosote. Unlike almost all equipment procured by the military, these sleds had no distinctive markings such as military serial numbers or "U.S." This particular sled was used extensively by many units throughout the military, including these at Camp Hale, Camp Rimini, Newfoundland, and Greenland. At Chinook Kennels during the early years of the war they were even mounted with .30-caliber machine guns.[12]

Much of the testing and development of military sleds was done during the early part of World War II at Camp Hale, Colorado, under the direction of the Mountain and Winter Warfare Board at the Mountain Training Center, in conjunction with formation of the Tenth Mountain Division. Influenced by the Finns' experience in their "Winter War" with Russia, during this period the U.S. Army looked at every aspect of dog team transport. A major part of the conceptual investigation was to determine if dog teams could successfully support a division-size organization in an Arctic or mountain environment.[13] In early 1943 the Mountain and Winter Warfare Board decided that dogsleds were no longer to be considered for large-scale use.[14] This decision alone relegated dogsleds to "nonstandard" status because of the limited need for them.

The testing done during this period determined that the sleds available were not adequate for mountain warfare. 2nd Lt. Stuart A. Mace later said that the Wonalancet sled was the best and that "it might have worked at the South Pole—not with the mountain and ski troops." The primary problem in the deep powder snow of Colorado was that narrow runners sank, causing sleds to bog down. And any attempt to sidehill (go across the slope) on steep terrain required considerable finesse and luck to prevent sleds from tipping over and spilling their loads. Under Mace's leadership, two military dogsleds were manufactured at Camp Hale. Designed and built by the K-9 Detachment of the Mountain Training Center, these sleds were an attempt to overcome problems in mountainous regions. The first sled built was designated the "all purpose dog sled" or "standard mountain sled," then later known as the "Camp Hale sled." The sleds were crafted by Ed Moody (a former New England sled builder) at the Groswald Ski Company in nearby Denver.[15] The army standard mountain sled prototype

FIGURE 6.6. Camp Hale sled. (Courtesy of Lynne Mace)

was ten feet in overall length. Like the Wonalancet sled it was copied from, the Camp Hale sled was a five-stanchion basket type. This very innovative sled was not a combination sled-toboggan like the Wonalancet but had wide skilike runners (four and a half inches) to enable the sled to float on the surface of soft snow. The runners were steel edged like skis as well, for greater control on slick, icy slopes. A "keel" also ran the full length of the runners. On hardpack snow these keels supported the sled, eliminating the extra drag caused by wider ski runners. The keels also helped control the sled while traversing hills by acting as "slew" brakes (steel rudderlike appendages attached to the bottom of the runners). This type of runner was described as similar to "a ski with an ice skate down the middle." Because of the wide runners, the sled itself was wider (twenty-six inches) than other sleds of the time, which averaged twenty-two inches, so it was even more stable. The original sled was equipped with a gee pole bracket and slew brakes, but they disappeared on later adaptations. The sled weighed only seventy-three pounds. [16] Though it had only limited testing at Camp Hale in May 1943, it was considered superior to all other sleds tested in stability, load carrying capacity, and ease of towing. [17]

The convertible sled previously mentioned as described in FM 25-6 was also extensively tested and modified by the Mountain Training Center. It is incorrectly thought of by most people today as *the* army dogsled. The actual nomenclature was "sled-toboggan, convertible, general purpose, 400 pound capacity." Weighing only thirty-six pounds, it was primarily designed to be hauled by men on skis and snowshoes, but it could also be used with a dog team. It was really a combination sled-toboggan that could easily be changed from one mode to the other, leading to the common term *convertible*. The bed of the seven-foot, five-inch sled was constructed from half-inch maple plywood, supported by six plywood uprights on three-inch-wide runners. By unscrewing four fastening devices, these runners could be repositioned to lie flat against the bed, creating a toboggan. Because the upper structure could be easily disassembled for shipping, it was also known as the collapsible sled. In its original contractual configuration, dog experts considered this sled inadequate for dog team use in spite of the large numbers built for the army. It was totally rebuilt by Ed Moody at the Groswald Ski Company to increase its utility and eliminate some of the more objectionable features. The six supports were changed to eight, making the sled stronger. Originally the sled runners extended only four inches to the rear of the sled, which gave a person on snowshoes plenty of clearance to help direct the sled but was too short for a dog driver to stand on. Runners were extended by five inches to afford foot room for dog drivers. A hinged brake was also added, as well as a brush bow or "bushwhacker," as it was called in the original test report to the Quartermaster General. Slew brakes similar to those on the standard mountain sled were also added to the runners. The plow type handles were discarded, as was the rear bulkhead type structure, and replaced with three stanchion-supported removable handles, which gave the sled-toboggan the look of a real dogsled. With these modifications the sled more nearly approached an all-purpose carrier, but it still failed to approximate the efficiency of the army standard mountain sled. Because it was only twenty inches wide, the convertible sled tipped over easily. Snow also tended to pack against the support uprights owing to their width, their close spacing, and the abrupt upturn of the front end. After modifications it weighed sixty-four pounds, almost as much as the original standard mountain sled. Its primary advantages were that it was easily transported because of removable side rails and that it could be built in quantity for approximately $100.[18] The standard, unmodified version was marked in typical military fashion with Quartermaster contract numbers, serial numbers, manufacturer, and "U.S." and was painted white for camouflage. The modified version was never produced under contract. Although the illustration in *FM 70-15, Operations in Snow and Extreme Cold* (November 1944) depicts a modified version with a foot brake and extended runners, it does not approach the radical changes of the Camp Hale version. A report depicting the modified convertible sled-toboggan and the army standard mountain sled was submitted to the Quartermaster General, proposing that the former be adopted throughout the army. It was also forwarded to Sir George Hubert Wilkins, James Ford, and Roy Teller, "experts on dog problems" who were serving as civilian advisers in the War Department. [19]

The K-9 Detachment from the Mountain Training Center at Camp Hale, Colorado, was eventually transferred to Camp Rimini, Montana (the War Dog Reception Center) in June 1943, taking not only dogs, drivers, instructors, and sleds but also all the knowledge and experience gained up to that time. Camp Rimini in time became the sled-building center for the U.S. military. Standards for sleds that had almost been achieved at Camp Hale were abandoned during this period, mainly because the dog unit at Rimini was not run as a "spit and polish" military organization and because the sled builders and mushers were always trying to build a better sled. [20]

John A. Matovich (an army sled builder at Camp Rimini) explained: "Builders added features requested by drivers. We also got feedback from active units in the field that utilized equipment which promoted changes and new sled designs." Steam-bending equipment at the sled shop let sled builders usually build one sled a week. In the two years that the sled shop operated, over one hundred sleds were constructed. There were six sled builders who worked full time at the shop, and soldier drivers also spent time helping out there. Drivers were especially interested in learning about sled construction, particularly the rawhide lashings, to help them make repairs in the field. [21]

At Camp Rimini, the army standard mountain sled became nonstandard, and in the "new" nomenclature it became the "Camp Hale sled." Its overall basic design was maintained but continued to be improved on. It was built in various lengths from eight to sixteen feet. Runners varied from the wide ski type to more traditional two-inch widths. [22] The Tenth Mountain Division was out of the dogsled mode of transportation by this time, so the need for mountain runners diminished because most sleds were bound for search and rescue squadrons operating in Newfoundland and Greenland. Narrow-runner sleds were more than adequate for the icy and more level terrain in

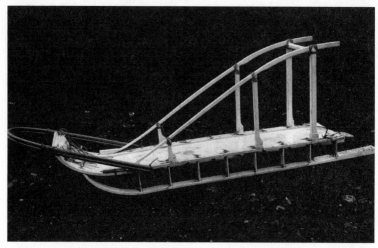

FIGURE 6.7. Modified sled-toboggan. Even with all the changes, this sled was still convertible to a toboggan. (Courtesy of Lynne Mace)

those locations, so sleds were lighter and easier to construct. The original Camp Hale sled was bolted or screwed together, but the Camp Rimini versions were lashed together, as a result either of more testing or of experience garnered from others. The sled that was tested at Camp Hale did not even have any cross lashings between stanchions. The lashed versions were more flexible, so they could better withstand the rigors of use without breaking. The original Camp Hale sled was less stalwart than later versions that were built at Camp Rimini. Stanchions were thinner than in the Camp Rimini version and were attached to the runners using eyebolts and lashings instead of inserted through holes drilled in the runners and fastened with lashings. The Camp Rimini version increased in overall weight to 115 pounds. The collapsing gee pole socket of the earlier version also disappeared.

One of the descendants of the Camp Hale sled was called the Bagby-Johnson sled. It was built based on requirements of two army mushers in Alaska, hence its name, and was designed to be used on Alaskan tundra. It was twelve feet, six inches long, with six stanchions and narrow inch-and-a-half runners, and was very supple. It weighed approximately 100 pounds. These sleds were used by the navy (with army drivers and dogs from Camp Rimini) to survey the Naval Petroleum Reserves at Point Barrow. When the project was finished, army drivers returned to Camp Rimini with only dogs and harnesses. Navy officers took the sleds with them as souvenirs after the operation terminated.[23]

Another design that was produced from the Camp Hale version was the "Presque Isle sled," built with specifications provided by Maj. Norman D. Vaughn of the First Arctic Search and Rescue Squadron. It was eleven feet long, with narrow runners and five stanchions, similar to the Camp Hale sled. About a dozen were built and shipped to squadron headquarters at Presque Isle, Maine.[24]

Some other sled modifications were made mostly for aesthetic reasons. Instead of the rear cross bracing of more "standard" versions, many mushers liked a bent wooden circle or a combination of the two. There was no real purpose for this design. The military justified this purely individualistic variation as good for morale and as encouraging the builders' pride in their work. The cross bracing was considered stronger than the circle bracing.[25]

One of the more unusual variations of the Camp Hale sled made at Camp Rimini used ax handles for stanchions. The idea came from Major Vaughn because wood for repairs was scarce. Since ax handles were standard issue within military supply channels, they were readily available. The sled was an incredible fifteen feet long, designed to span massive crevasses encountered in Greenland if a snowbridge collapsed. Its runners were two inches wide, and the ten stanchions were fabricated from U.S. Army ax handles. The sled was designed for a payload of a ton and weighed 185 pounds itself. In spite of its size and weight, it was still pulled by a standard dog team. It was called "Big Bertha" or "Tikky Bear" after the huge railway guns of World War I.[26]

The collapsible or convertible sled resurfaced again at Camp Rimini. The Arctic explorer Sir Hubert Wilkins built several very sophisticated plywood versions of the collapsible sled and brought them to the camp for comparison testing in April 1943. Photographs of sleds taken at the Gould Diggings area on Red Mountain at Camp Rimini show a more augmented version than Mace's and Moody's adaptation. Sled driver Dave Armstrong stated, "The sleds were very stout. In spite of our efforts, we were unable to break them." These sleds were developed to be parachuted from search planes to downed air crews.[27] In spite of Wilkins's reputation as a polar expert, his recommendations for dogsleds were never adopted.

Camp Rimini closed down in the spring of 1944, when limited use of dog teams could not justify a separate facility. Sled builders, equipment, mush-

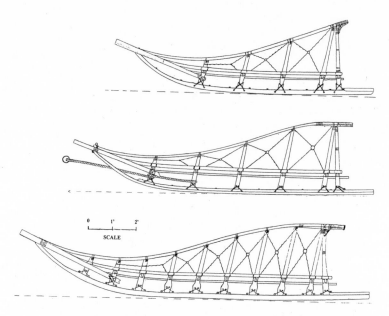

FIGURE 6.8. Comparison of the Presque Isle sled (*top*), the Bagby-Johnson sled (*middle*), and "Big Bertha" (*bottom*). (Original drawings by Stuart Mace)

ers, and dogs were again displaced, this time to Fort Robinson, Nebraska. Sleds were still built there until the end of the war and demobilization, but no significant sled changes or developments were made. Sleds still in active service at demobilization were often given to local indigenous peoples in order to clear property books.

The U.S. Army continued to look at sled development after the war when the opportunity arose. There was even a brief report written in 1948 by an army observer on the Ronne Antarctic research expedition. The army had totally forgotten all its years of expertise in the art and science of dogsleds and was back to looking at the basic Antarctic sled that polar explorer Fridtjof Nansen had developed years before. Conclusions regarding dogsleds reached during the expedition regurgitated the same lessons learned during World War II. These suggestions included:

1. Plastic-sheathed runners are superior to either metal or wood. Of the latter two, metal is superior to wood on wet snow and corn snow. Wood

is superior on cold, dry, wind packed snow. [Use of plastic was the only real "new" information discovered.]

2. Coating of wooden runners with several layers of ice is a decided help in temperature below 20 degrees.

3. If metal runners are used, they should be of one-piece construction.

4. Plywood should be used instead of hickory wherever it does not interfere with flexibility.

5. Rawhide lashing is the best method of combining strength and flexibility at joints.

6. A springboard-toothed brake at the rear is essential.

7. There is a need to prevent sideslip on icy slopes.

8. Gee poles and handlebars are necessary. They should be collapsible for military purposes, and preferably of light metal.

9. Sleds that float, and waterproof sled tanks to protect the load, are an advantage on sea ice.[28]

After the war, dog teams stayed as part of U.S. Air Force rescue units operating in northern areas. With experiments in aerial delivery techniques such as parachuting, "real" dogsleds were almost all replaced with the convertible sled-toboggan, because it was widely available and inexpensive. These sleds were maintained in the air force inventory until they were displaced by the helicopter in the mid-1950s. Sleds, like the sled dogs themselves, had no future in a modern U.S. Air Force.

7. Sled Dogs Save Lives

Search and Rescue

Dog teams were used for search and rescue missions in the Arctic even before the United States entered World War II. Aircraft being ferried to Europe under the Lend-Lease program used a route from Presque Isle, Maine, across northeastern Canada at Goose Bay, Newfoundland, to Greenland, to Iceland, and on to Prestwick, Scotland. Col. Brent Balchen, a noted polar aviation explorer, began his appointment as commander of Task Force Eight in 1941. The task force's mission was to create a link on the west coast of Greenland at Narsarssuak. In addition to founding the ferrying route, Balchen was responsible for establishing weather stations, patrolling the entire coast of Greenland, and protecting the country from enemy action.[1] Balchen's own experiences in polar regions had emphasized the importance of sled dogs for ground travel. He had used dog teams in the early 1930s to set up a rescue network for Admiral Richard E. Byrd's historic flight over the South Pole in case he was forced down. Balchen relied heavily on his experience to design the North Atlantic rescue system. To initiate the Greenland operation, he procured thirty-five sled dogs from Arthur Walden's Chinook Kennels in Wonalancet, New Hampshire, along with two half-breed timber wolves.[2] These animals provided the basis for search and rescue operations that evolved into the paramount mission for sled dog teams during the war.

When the North Atlantic Division of the Army Air Force Air Transportation Command (AAFTC) demonstrated that it could fly the North Atlantic route at any time, it became clear that land search and rescue units had to be established to supplement existing air and sea rescue units. Land units were needed to retrieve downed aviators from the hardest, most desolate terrain on earth, a remote wilderness stretching millions of square miles north, beyond the Arctic Circle.

Before units were officially formed, rescues depended on dog teams assembled using local assets. Commanders rented or leased teams, or else they enlisted well-known people such as Maj. Norman D. Vaughn and navy lieutenant Freddy Crockett, both former Antarctic dog handlers. Vaughn and Crockett frequently performed rescues and other functions, sometimes using their own dog teams.[3]

In one famous incident, two B-17 bombers and five P-38 fighter aircraft being ferried to Europe made forced landings on a glacier after encountering bad weather and running low on fuel. Twenty-five men were stranded on the ice, the largest single stranding of airmen in World War II. At Norman Vaughn's insistence, the army air force asked for help from Freddy Crockett, then stationed with the navy on Greenland's east coast with his own dog team. For this rescue, Vaughn was allowed to collect six of his own dogs that were in Boston. While Vaughn was assembling his team, Crockett started out alone. Guided only by an aircraft, Crockett navigated eighteen miles of crevasse-riven terrain to reach the stranded crew. When he reached the men, he guided them back across the dangerous area to the coast, where they were picked up by a coast guard boat. In the excitement, the crew of one of the B-17s had forgotten to destroy its Norden bomb sight, so Vaughn and Max Demerest, a skier, were dispatched back through the same treacherous area to recover the secret device, since all the aircraft were in full view of any ships cruising nearby. On the return trip the dog team had to be moved up a two-hundred-foot ice wall. The men hauled the dogs to the top one at a time by ropes attached to their harnesses, then they hauled equipment, supplies, and sled up the cliff the same way. When a violent storm slowed them down, Vaughn and Demerest could not get to the aircraft in the allotted time. Demerest returned to the coast to tell the rendezvous boat to wait, since the rescuers had no radio contact with their base. Vaughn continued to the crash location alone with his dog team and spent a tense night removing the bomb sight. He imagined that every creak and groan from the abandoned aircraft was a German landing party. Two days later he joined Demerest again, and they made their way back to the ship, after eleven harrowing days. They brought the bomb sight out right under the noses of German submarines lurking in the area. After this mission, recovery of aircraft and equipment became another facet of search and rescue operations.[4]

Dog teams were key elements in an amazing Arctic rescue in 1942, when an aircraft crashed in Greenland only twenty-five miles from a weather and rescue station. Its crew of nine men had no Arctic survival equipment or training. A local dog team was sent but could not get through the deep, soft snow to reach the crash site. Search aircraft dropped food and survival equipment, allowing crew members to survive harsh conditions, but storms and poor weather stymied more than an occasional resupply flight. Twenty days later an aircraft was finally able to land nearby, and the two most seriously injured men were taken out. Another rescue aircraft was flying out a third survivor when it crashed, killing all on board. An Eskimo dog team later recovered the bodies of this group. In renewed ground rescue attempts using motor sledges (the forerunner of snowmobiles), Max Demerest was killed when his motor sledge was swallowed up by a crevasse. The crew was finally rescued an incredible 129 days later. Three dog teams plowed through deep snow to the crash site, guided by an aircraft using radio signals. These teams were led by Captain Harold Strong, an Alaskan, and Sergeants Joseph Heally and "Dutch" Dolleman, both of whom had served with Byrd in Antarctica. Remaining crew members were shuttled by dog team to the sled camp, where an aircraft was able to land and carry them to safety. This rescue has been called one of the great sagas of the Arctic.[5] Without rescue by dog team, these men would surely have perished in the cold only a short distance from safety.

Many rescues unfortunately turned out to be primarily body recoveries. Vaughn often searched wrecks that had crashed long before, and also crash sites found by local people. In one incident Vaughn hired two dog teams and native drivers to find a B-26 bomber that had left for Narsarssuak on December 8, 1942, but never arrived. After locating the aircraft, they recovered the bodies of four crew members who had died from starvation. They later learned that four other crewmen had tried unsuccessfully to float down the coast to Goose Bay.[6]

It was due to the early successes of people like Vaughn and Crockett that Arctic Search and Rescue Squadrons were formed to provide dedicated search and rescue capability. Norman Vaughn was the commander of the First Arctic Search and Rescue Squadron, created in 1943.[7] After these units were officially formed, there were twenty-nine dog teams spread throughout the north country from northern Maine to Labrador, Baffin Island, Newfoundland, and Iceland. Sled dog teams were not the only dogs trained for the Arctic Search and Rescue Squadrons. Saint Bernards and a few other breeds such as Labradors and Great Pyrenees were trained to work as pack

FIGURE 7.1. Sled dogs being transported in C-47 aircraft.
(Courtesy of Lynne Mace)

dogs and also to pull pulkas—small boatlike sleds designed to transport several hundred pounds of load or carry a person through thick undergrowth where a dog team would find it hard to move. In addition to sled dogs and pack dogs, Arctic Search and Rescue Squadrons had all the newest types of over-snow equipment available during the latter part of the war, including the weasel (a type of snowcat), early snowmobiles called motor sledges, and tractors equipped with tracks and skis on the front axle. But it was the dog teams that in one way or another accounted for most rescues and recoveries.[8]

Arctic Search and Rescue Squadrons were organized into Flights A, B, C, and D, consisting of 164 officers and soldiers per flight who ranged from pilots and aircraft repair specialists to dog team drivers and handlers.[9] A total of 108 dogs were assigned to the squadron, 36 each to Flights B, C, and D.[10] According to the *Table of Organization and Equipment* (TOE), each flight was authorized to have six basket sleds and six convertible toboggan-sleds, which were listed as nonstandard items (not available through normal supply channels). Each flight was to have four dog team kits that would each equip a standard hitch of nine dogs. Kits consisted of nine sets of "Siwash" low-back draft harnesses, a gangline, a tethering line, combination kennel and choke-collar chains, and a dog whip.[11] Transport and light utility aircraft, gliders, and a helicopter were all assets assigned to the organization,[12] demonstrating the unusual combinations required for search and rescue of downed fliers.

Dog drivers were considered noncombatants because of their rescue function, but according to the TOE they were assigned weapons (U.S. .30-caliber MI carbines).[13] Most drivers did not normally carry weapons, however. After one nasty incident in Newfoundland, the commander ordered all drivers to carry their assigned weapons whenever they were driving their dogs. The team was attacked not by an offshore German submarine or landing party but by civilian oxen pulling a load of wood that went berserk as a dog team passed by. The oxen tore into the dog team, injuring several dogs and totally wrecking the sled. Thereafter all men were required to carry their weapons for self-defense. Rifles were also handy for hunting snowshoe hares and ptarmigan to supplement rations. Driver David W. Armstrong Jr. told me, "It was difficult to hit hares zigzagging through the snow, but it sure provided a lot of entertainment."[14]

M.Sgt. Richard S. Moulton (the primary person responsible for the army sled dog program at Camp Rimini) later served in the search and rescue unit at Goose Bay, Labrador. On one mission, two rescue teams each made up of nine dogs and two sleds were dispatched to find a downed Canadian B-24 bomber. When Moulton arrived at the isolated crash site one crew member was already dead. Another was flown out by a small single-engine aircraft. The dogsleds guided the remaining crew members back to Goose Bay along the frozen Hamilton River through desolate borderlands.[15] Once a crash was located, the primary task of dog drivers was either to get crewmen to an area where they could be picked up by aircraft or to guide them back to civilization. Unless they were injured, fliers often had to walk out following the sled tracks. Dogs had enough to do pulling the load of food and other supplies needed for party's survival during the long trek home. ˙

Dave Armstrong (who had worked at Chinook Kennels and was deeply involved in army dogsledding from its inception) spent over three years as a dog driver and trainer with the Quartermaster Corps and the U.S. Army Air Force. Besides service at Camp Rimini, he was assigned to Presque Isle, Maine, and Harmon Field, Stephenville, and Gander in Newfoundland, all remote outposts. Most of Armstrong's missions were body recoveries. There was little excitement in the work once they found the aircraft. During the search, adrenaline and the hope of saving lives kept rescuers going, but gathering remains was mentally and physically exhausting. On one exacting search for a missing B-24 bomber they searched an area for twenty-one days. The plane was finally located by a local trapper who first spotted a shirt in a tree, then a detached leg, and finally the aircraft. Two dog teams were sent out from Gander, fifteen air miles away, to recover not only the crew but also new, particularly secret radar equipment on board the aircraft. The team recovered all the bodies and equipment and returned them to its base at Gander Field.[16]

On another rigorous mission Armstrong, accompanied by two other drivers (Willard E. Gregg and Truman Watson) and pack dog handler Carl F. Lowe, was sent to recover the cargo of a crashed C-54 transport plane. They recovered 5,800 pounds of cargo and thirty-two sacks of mail from the crash site in isolated mountains above Codroy Pond, Newfoundland. The teams brought the complete cargo down to the railhead in only two days. Lowe's five Saint Bernard pack dogs were hitched to a basket sled to help pull loads. The entire contingent of sled dog teams and pack dogs went back up the mountain and helped the salvage crew carry as much of the aircraft as could be saved down the mountain, including a dual landing gear weighing 2,800 pounds. The landing gear had to be lashed to the sled with the two wheels trailing behind. This sled was pulled by a team of dogs whose total weight was only 495 pounds. For the steep downhill portion of the trip, the load had to be unhitched and belayed with two hundred feet of five-eighths-inch rope wrapped around a tree. On flat terrain, where the wheel would not roll on its own, dogs were again harnessed to it. Other equipment that dog teams hauled out on this mission included the 1,500-pound nose gear, propellers, and propeller gearing. Five propeller blades were taken out on one load; then on another trip seven blades that had been bent were dragged behind the team with a rope.[17] Wrestling such heavy loads down the mountain was extremely labor intensive and dangerous. Drivers sometimes narrowly missed serious injuries when they were smashed between bulky loads and trees as sleds slid off the trail.

Each mission for search and rescue teams was quite different. Though the average length of missions involving dog teams was approximately four days, some were incredibly long ordeals. The fastest rescue time was three

FIGURE 7.2. Search and rescue dog team at the site of a C-54 crash at Codroy Pond, Newfoundland, 1944. This is one of few photos of crashes that survived military censorship. Dog drivers Carl F. Lowe, Truman C. Watson, and Willard E. Gregg on left. The Lead dog is Togo. (Dave Armstrong. Photo computer enhanced by Mike Jones)

hours, when a pilot crashed not far off the end of the runway at a base in Greenland.[18]

When teams were not performing rescues, the unit constantly underwent arduous and challenging training under Major Vaughn's supervision. One exercise-demonstration, a simulated rescue, was conducted in the White Mountains of New Hampshire. With ten feet of snow, subzero temperatures, and winds of fifty-five miles an hour to deal with, rescue crews found and treated a simulated injured pilot, then transported him back to home base. Part of the exercise required that the injured pilot, along with the sled, dog team, and driver, be lowered with ropes down an eighty-foot ice-covered cliff face.[19] The crew lowered them all safely by rigging a Tyrolean traverse (a sophisticated overhead suspension system constructed of mountaineering rope). This maneuver was a spectacular public relations finale for the exercise, captured by news cameras and with live radio commentary.

FIGURE 7.3. Sled dogs being lowered down a Tyrolean traverse during White Mountains training exercise. (National Archives III-SC-329100)

One of the least-known attempted rescue missions involving dog teams occurred in the European Theater of Operations (ETO), during the Battle of the Bulge. Deep snow was severely hampering evacuation of wounded soldiers during the German offensive. Norman Vaughn suggested that dog teams could be used to transport the wounded from forward areas to battalion aid stations. As with many ideas that had never been tried before, the military upper echelon failed to react favorably to the suggestion. It was not until Gen. George Patton himself heard of the plan that it was approved— thirty days after it was proposed. Finally four C-54 aircraft were assigned to transport 209 sled dogs, seventeen dog drivers, and two sleds per team, plus all the other necessary equipment including dog food and rations for a thirty-day mission. Within four days of mission approval, personnel, dogs, and equipment were gathered from locations all over the North Atlantic to be flown to Le Bourget airfield near Paris. Aircraft were supposed to land at Iceland en route but could not do so because of threatening weather. To avoid the ominous weather, the pilots climbed to twenty thousand feet, causing all the dogs and passengers to pass out from oxygen deprivation in the nonpressurized cabins. The flight crews had oxygen but did not share it with the dog drivers.[20] To make the snafu more acceptable to those who

FIGURE 7.4. Some of the sled dogs and drivers in France during the Battle of the Bulge. (National Archives III-SC-200743)

heard about the incident later, it was said to have been done deliberately to stop the dogs from fighting.[21] Once in France, teams were divided and sent to two locations. Half the teams, under the command of Major Vaughn, were flown by C-47 to within five miles of the front on the France-Belgium border. The other group, commanded by Capt. Bill Shearer, was flown to Belgium. Other participants in the mission were M.Sgt. Dick Moulton, Cpl. George Esslinger, S.Sgt. Roy Billings, Sgt. John Shand, S.Sgt. John Wanks, Sgt. Hazzard H. Ruland, Sgt. Paul Becker, Sgt. Cletus Barbeau, Sgt. Willard E. Gregg, Sgt. Truman C. Watson, S.Sgt. Louis Colombo, S.Sgt. Robert J. Lucy, S.Sgt. Huel S. Dean, Pfc. Arthur B. Bacon, Capt. Donald Shaw, and Lt. Peter Hostmark.[22]

The dogs and men spent thirty days in the ETO and conducted many demonstrations using dogsleds, showing that each team of nine dogs could carry one patient litter per sled and another litter on a trailer sled. Drivers decided among themselves that they would use only four dogs per sled and would lead them instead of riding behind in the usual fashion. Dogs were kept in shape by pulling an old automobile chassis around the staging area every day. Because military staff had delayed mission approval so long, the mission ultimately failed. During the postponement heavy snow changed to rain

FIGURE 7.5. Sled dogs and sleds on airfield in France during the Battle of the Bulge. The sled in the foreground is the Wonalancet type. (National Archives III-SC-200745)

and mud, a poor environment for sled dogs. The dogs and men never got to prove their capabilities; they never evacuated one wounded soldier while they were in Europe.[23]

Search and rescue operations were going on in Alaska at the same time. They were simply less well known than those in the North Atlantic. The rescue squadrons of the Alaskan Wing of the Air Transport Command maintained dogs for rescues involving aircraft flying across Alaska to Russia and across the Bering Strait to Siberia under the Lend-Lease program. The route began at Great Falls, Montana, crossed Canada to Ladd Field at Fairbanks, Alaska, then went on to Siberia via Galena and Nome, Alaska. It covered an area easily as desolate as the North Atlantic route.

Men and dogs of search and rescue squadrons effectively retrieved approximately 150 survivors, 300 casualties, and millions of dollars worth of equipment by the close of World War II. Many saves are credited to dogs and mushers in Canada, Alaska, Newfoundland, and Greenland.[24]

Rescue units supported by sled dogs continued to operate through the mid-1950s, long after the war was over. Frequently, civilian dog teams were contracted to penetrate the Arctic to perform rescue and recovery missions, just like many missions in World War II. Joe Reddington (known as the father of the Iditarod) was contracted on numerous occasions for "reclamation" (recovery of salvageable equipment from crashed aircraft). All usable parts were hauled away to pickup sites by dog teams, then what remained of the aircraft had to be buried so it would not be reported as a "fresh" find if sighted again.[25]

An intriguing incident occurred when Sgt. Orvin L. Haugan (who was with the Tenth Rescue Squadron in Alaska in 1946) was air landed with his dog team to rescue the crew of a downed C-47. Engine problems had forced the C-47 to land in the barren wilderness of the Yukon Territory, so a CG-15 glider landed Sergeant Haugan and his rescue dog team on a nearby frozen lake. The uninjured crew was evacuated by dogsled and picked up by aircraft at the improvised lake runway. A complete aircraft engine was flown in, and Haugan's sled team carried it in piece by piece, along with mechanics, to repair the C-47. Finally, a month and a half later (after it had been totally overhauled in the wilderness), the aircraft was flown out. Haugan and his dogs remained on location during this entire time to help transport supplies and parts from the lake landing area to the aircraft site. Haugan also had to act as nursemaid for the mechanics, using his woodsman's skills to provide back-country living accommodations and serving as camp cook. Since the glider had already been retrieved by a tugline snatch, the whole group, including the dogs, was eventually evacuated and flown out by a Norseman bush plane.[26]

The unpleasant task of body recovery was still a major focus of many missions by search and rescue squadrons after the war. As late as 1955, dog teams were still used by U.S. Air Force pararescue units until all were replaced by helicopters. In one of the last rescues supported by dog teams in Alaska, dogs were flown in by helicopter to a navy PV-2 Neptune patrol aircraft crash site on Mount Susitna near Anchorage. Operating in twelve-foot snow, the rescue team took forty-two days to retrieve the bodies of eleven crew members. The dog team was used exclusively for body recovery, except for general hauling around the camps. The dogs themselves often located remains by their keen senses.[27]

These are just a few incidents out of hundreds of rescues and recoveries that owed their success to determined men and dogs from Arctic Search

FIGURE 7.6. S.Sgt. Orvin L. Haugan, Polar School, Kotzebue Sound, Alaska, in January 1948. (Courtesy of Eugene Armstrong, Pararescue Association)

and Rescue Squadrons. Never standing still, these units were always looking for better, faster, more efficient ways to perform their jobs. Experiments with parachute delivery of sled dog teams were common until dogs and drivers were replaced by the helicopter. Dogs still in service at that time were sold cheap, most for only $10. Dogs tracing their lineage back to Leonard Seppala's dogs (Seppala was a famous Alaskan sled dog racer) sold for upward of $90. One officer in Alaska proposed to dispose of these loyal dogs by shooting them. [28] Many sleds were casually given away to local native residents. By the time using helicopters became standard procedure in postwar search and rescue endeavors, tough and reliable sled dogs had disappeared without fanfare from U.S. military service.

On November 11, 1948, Brent Balchen (former commander of Task Force Eight and the architect for the original dog-team-oriented rescue system) took over command of the Tenth Rescue Squadron in Alaska. On assuming command, he stated that "whirlybirds are superior even to dog teams."[29] But he later lamented that he would especially miss hearing the dogs sing late at night. In his heart he was still a dog man.

8. "Grrronimo!"

Sled Dogs Hit the Silk

The primary use of sled dog teams within the U.S. military was search and rescue operations to recover air crews downed in the Arctic. During World War II thousands of aircraft were ferried over both the North Atlantic route and the Alaska–Siberia route. All the portions of the routes that passed over land crossed remote Arctic and subarctic terrain, where ground travel was almost nonexistent. Starting in 1943 the U.S. Army Air Corps began forming Arctic Search and Rescue Squadrons, the forerunner of modern-day pararescue units. These units were strategically deployed along the two routes, using sled dog teams for ground rescue.

Generally downed crews were first located by air, and survival equipment was dropped to sustain them until they could be recovered. Sled dog teams were then dispatched overland, and arrival time depended on distance and weather. Since rescue times could be greatly shortened if rescue teams got there sooner, the army air corps soon experimented with parachuting dogs, drivers, and sleds to crash sites.[1] Early attempts by the First Arctic Search and Rescue Squadron in Newfoundland used improvised equipment, then more sophisticated gear was developed and tested at Camp Rimini.

Maj. Norman D. Vaughn (commander of the First Search and Rescue Squadron) was one of the first to conduct these experiments. He first dropped a dummy dog made of wood and sandbags, but the parachute failed to open. The dummy weighed only twenty-five pounds, not heavy enough to open the cargo 'chute. Vaughn continued to solve problems that arose and eventually did successful live drops. The first actual parachute rescue operation was at the Grenfell Mission at St. Anthony, Newfoundland. Dr. Wilfred Grenfell was a medical missionary who ministered to remote Indian villages in the region by dogsled. When all his dogs died during a distemper epidemic, he sent out a call for assistance. During a civic action program under the direction of Major Vaughn, ten U.S. Army sled dogs were dropped without any injuries. One dog did land in the water, but it was immediately fished out by a crash rescue boat that had been standing by to support the operation. [2]

For Major Vaughn's early parachute drops, no special equipment was designed for the dogs. The military sled dog harness made from one-inch cotton webbing was simply attached to a small cargo parachute, with the dogs' hind legs looped through the side straps to provide support and keep them from falling out of the harness. [3] As others experimented with parachute delivery techniques, special harnesses were developed. At Major Vaughn's request, Lt. Stuart A. Mace also began work on parachuting dogs at Camp Rimini. Mace's research on developing packs for dogs directly related to parachute harnesses as well, because knowing dog anatomy was the key to proper fitting. [4]

There was no parachute tower available for testing equipment without making live drops from aircraft, though such towers were found at military parachute schools at Fort Benning, Georgia, and Fort Bragg, North Carolina. Therefore the Camp Rimini staff built one by stripping two uniformly tapered lodgepole pines of their limbs and stretching a cable between them that supported a spring and pulley device in midspan. Because the dogs might be injured, only culled dogs were used for testing—dogs that for one reason or another could not be issued as sled dog replacements but had not been condemned to be destroyed. Dogs were hauled up the mock tower with the aid of pulleys and allowed to free-fall for twenty feet, when the drop would be arrested with springs to simulate the opening shock of the parachute, just as with the thirty-four-foot towers used at army parachute training centers. The dog suspended in its harness would then be lowered to the ground. [5]

Several harness designs were tested. The best was a vest of heavy cotton duck lined with sheepskin and incorporating parachute webbing, similar to the rigs worn by humans. These harnesses were attached to a twenty-four-foot 'chute—the same type (with slight modifications) that paratroopers used as a reserve parachute—as recommended by the parachute school at Fort Benning, Georgia. The school also made some other technical recommendations. One harness that had been used successfully to drop a mascot dog at Fort Benning was sent to Camp Rimini for study. [6] The harness that

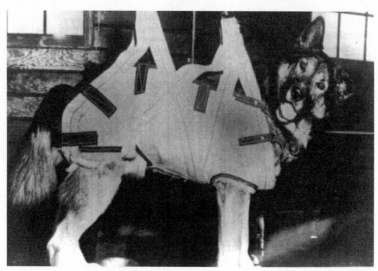

FIGURE 8.1. Dog wearing Rimini dog parachute harness at San Carlos, California. (National Archives 111-SC-133671)

evolved from all these studies was called the Rimini dog parachute harness. It had three major design features. It was meant to give dogs the greatest possible protection against the shock of parachute opening; it was to land dogs in a position that would lessen the chance of injury; and it was designed to prevent dogs from slipping out of the harness during jumps.[7] Sample harnesses were supplied by request to the San Carlos War Dog Reception and Training Center in California, the Quartermaster General in Washington DC, and the Rescue Officer, Alaskan Wing, at Edmonton, Canada.[8]

The major problem Mace encountered was the landing. Paratroopers are taught to "tuck and roll" on landing, executing what has become known as a PLF (parachute landing fall) to prevent broken bones, but dogs could not be taught the technique. The harness was designed so the dogs' rear legs hit the ground first to better absorb landing shock. It was also decided to have two dogs jump together. Since sled dogs work in pairs, they could support each other. Reports cite no injuries to dogs during these early experiments.[9]

After initial tower tests at Camp Rimini in the spring of 1944, dogs were taken to Great Falls, Montana, where a Norseman aircraft from the rescue circuit was available for trials. The first drop used a single dog instead of a two-dog team, since the lead dog on a sled team might not tolerate being harnessed to another dog. Drops were originally made onto wheat fields around Great Falls, which were level but rough. The pilot slowed the aircraft to almost stall speed, then rolled it so the door opening was downward. Dogs were thrown straight out with considerable force by a dog handler who was tied into the plane. The parachute was opened by a static line, just like a paratrooper's. The after-action report of the initial drop said that the first dog dropped was "paralyzed with fright" on landing, but after being petted and talked to, he got to his feet as lively as ever. Of seven dogs parachuted, the first was the only one affected that way. The others were ready to go immediately upon landing. One dog jumped four times; he showed no fear on reentering the plane and gave no additional resistance to being tossed from the aircraft.[10]

The initial test drop was done from an altitude of 900 feet, but it was found that dogs could be safely dropped from only 350 feet, making it possible to hit a very small clearing.[11] Dogs were dropped to precise locations by first using small, bright-colored spotter parachutes. By watching where they landed, the pilot could compensate for wind drift. Dogs were pinpoint bombed to landing zones, and crew members on the ground would then collapse the 'chutes and gather up the dogs.[12]

Since drivers could be parachuted before dogs, the only other component of the dog team that needed delivery was the sled. Sleds were too long to fit into the fuselage of a Norseman, so they were lashed under the wing. Aircraft would dive-bomb target locations, and at the exact moment of pull-up, pilots would pull cords releasing the sled onto the snow without a parachute. Sleds were so well built that they all survived the landing without mishap.[13] No sled or sled dog was ever damaged in these early live tests, which were done in the Whitehorse area of the Yukon. During this same period, Canadian armed forces also contemplated parachuting dogs for rescue. They designed a dog parachute harness too, but the idea was scrapped when animal rights groups protested the plans.[14]

The Alaskan Wing of the Air Transport Command at Fort Nelson, Canada, rounded up seventeen dogs from Indians and other locals in the area to train for parachute operations. Maj. Joseph F. Westover (commander of the Canadian Sector Search and Rescue Unit) had little difficulty picking dogs for the initial test jump. He chose two dogs named Maggie and Jiggs, since they were the scrappiest of the bunch and always fighting. If anything went wrong, they were considered expendable. Maggie and Jiggs were attached

FIGURE 8.2. Sled dog wearing Rimini dog parachute harness during parachute descent in Alaska. (Courtesy of Francis M. Dawdy)

together in the two-dog technique with a twenty-eight-foot 'chute. They were thrown out at an altitude of 1,500 feet and landed without any problems. Strangely, the two dogs would get along without fighting only when they were flying or just after a parachute jump. These dogs were awarded parachute wings after making five successful jumps, the same number required for a human paratrooper.[15]

After the war, air force rescue units continued to develop techniques for parachuting sled dogs. The Seventy-first and Seventy-fourth Rescue Squadrons operating in Alaska trained frequently with parachute delivery systems. One air force pararescueman, Sgt. Francis M. Dawdy, jumped with sled dogs ten times and had no injuries to any dogs. After they landed, dogs were gathered up and hooked to a sled for a practice run. Dogs were relatively easy to round up, since their harnesses and attached parachutes prevented them from straying too far. Dawdy said, "Dogs had to be 'assisted' out the door, but once suspended under the canopy [they] seemed to enjoy the ride. They wagged their tails the whole time and became extremely excited every time they were strapped into their harnesses." In addition to parachuting, dogs were sometimes flown to landing sites and air landed. They then brought downed crew back to where they could be airlifted out. Troop transport gliders were also used to insert sled dogs into remote locations, saving travel time. Dogs were later taken out by gliders, using a tugline snatch by C-54 aircraft.[16] In this gut-wrenching procedure a glider's tow cable was stretched out in front of the aircraft with its end attached to a large loop suspended between two upright poles. A four-motor C-54 would launch the glider by making a low-level pass between the uprights to snag the loop with a hook trailing behind it.

It had been judged feasible to drop dogs and sleds to aircrews without also dropping a musher. The sled to be used was a collapsible sled-toboggan, sometimes called a converta-sled. Its relatively light weight (only thirty-six pounds) and the fact that all handles and rails disassembled for easy transport made it ideal for airborne delivery. The converta-sled had runners for use on hardpack snow, or it could be used as a toboggan in deep snow by changing the configuration of the runners. Designed to be towed by men on skis or snowshoes during World War II, the converta-sled was a poor substitute for a real dogsled. It was cheap, however, because it was made primarily from plywood, and it was available in great numbers. The master plan included dropping written instructions on basic dog driving with the dogs and sled so crews could evacuate themselves.[17] This concept never was put into practice, since enough pararescuemen became parachute qualified, by attending either the Army Airborne School at Fort Benning, Georgia, or the U.S. Forest Service Smoke Jumper School at Missoula, Montana.

The most bizarre technique for delivering dogs for rescue missions was dropping them into the snow without parachutes. This was tried in Greenland in 1952–53, where the winds were so fierce that an aircraft flying into the wind and throttled back with full flaps had an extremely slow ground speed.[18] Russians had used this method during the Russo-Finnish War to drop forces into deep snow from slow and extremely low-flying aircraft.[19] When one dog driver was briefed on the test procedure, he refused to drop his dogs without first jumping himself! This driver was described as a crusty old-time dog musher who cared deeply for his dogs and knew no fear. According to several accounts, Sgt. Leroy Lee Levigne made the jump with no injuries, then safely dropped his dogs in the same manner. The drop was made from a C-47 flying only twenty-five feet above the snow. Numerous test drops were made during that period, with three or four dogs dropped at a time. There were no reported injuries to any dogs. Pararescueman Levigne was subsequently court-martialed for his stunt and dismissed from the service under "Section Eight" (insanity), though he was later reinstated. Official records cannot be obtained to verify the incident because of the personnel action.[20]

As helicopters became more reliable, they too were used to transport sled dogs to crash sites. Thus the need to parachute dogs for rescue operations diminished. In fact, as their capabilities improved, helicopters replaced dog teams entirely, and sled dogs ultimately disappeared from U.S. Air Force inventory in the mid-1950s. With their demise, the commands "gee" and "haw" were no longer part of a rescueman's vocabulary. The excited yelps of "parapooches" were no longer heard when rescuemen jumped out the door of a perfectly sound airplane with the paratrooper's cry of "Geronimo!"

9. Sled Dogs in Summer

The Pack Dog Program

The U.S. Army pack dog program had its beginnings at Camp Hale, Colorado, as part of the original K-9 Detachment under the direction of the Mountain and Winter Warfare Board. The original intent was to train sled dog teams supporting the Tenth Mountain Division's invasion of Norway to work as pack dogs as well so they could still be useful in summer. [1] The program was redefined to include not only huskies but other breeds: Newfoundlands, Saint Bernards, Great Pyrenees, and Chesapeake Bay and Labrador retrievers. It was eventually determined that large northern dogs, such as mongrel Indian dogs and crossbred Mackenzie River huskies, were best suited for military pack dog operations in the Arctic. The pack dog program that began at Camp Hale was an integral part of the entire canine operation, even though it encompassed fewer dogs than sled dog programs at Camp Rimini and Fort Robinson. [2]

Dog packing is as old as dogsled driving, but few people were aware of it during the early part of World War II, and even fewer had any experience with it. In the Far North, Indians and Eskimos used their sled teams for packing in summer, improvising packs from hides and strapping. White fur traders and prospectors also used pack dogs, often considering them more useful than a sled team over rough land and tundra. The Arctic explorer Vilhjalmur Stefansson was one of very few others who touted the usefulness of pack dogs. [3] Because of lack of information and experience, the whole pack dog program was developed from scratch, including packs, training regimen, and doctrine. When the Camp Hale K-9 Detachment was shipped to Camp Rimini, 2nd Lt. Stuart A. Mace was given the assignment of developing a military pack dog program, [4] since there already was a higher-ranking officer (1st Lt. James Patenode) with sled dog experience in charge of sled dogs.

Sled dog drivers put up considerable resistance to working with pack dogs. According to Mace, "it was almost a snob resistance." There was much jealousy between the Sledge Dog Branch and the Pack Dog Branch, as the two groups had been divided. In a memorandum dated September 30, 1943, the commanding officer, Maj. E. J. Purfield, remarked: "Due to its size and numbers, the Sledge Dog Branch naturally takes precedence over the Pack Dog Branch. However, the absolute necessity of having a Pack Dog Branch . . . must not be overlooked and there should be no friction between the two." The two branches were located in different areas of the camp, but they often met on the trails during training. On one occasion a string of five Saint Bernards jumped into the middle of David W. Armstrong's sled team, causing a serious dogfight. While attempting to sort out the combatants, he saw his small female leader sitting quietly with her entire head in the huge mouth of one of the Saint Bernards.[5]

Because mushers resisted working in the pack dog program, many of its members were not dog drivers and so were considered unskilled by the sled dog cadre. One of these men was Pfc. Carl F. Lowe, who had no dog experience of any kind. "But this man had the patience to deal with anything," said Mace. Having no previous dealings with sled dogs, Lowe had no preconceived ideas about the superiority of driving them, making him ideal for the Pack Dog Branch. With large numbers of Great Pyrenees on hand, he was put in charge of training them and was finally able to train a group of six as pack dogs. Pfc. Robert W. Carroll, who had some experience with Saint Bernards, was put in charge of training them as well as Newfoundlands.[6] A very small contingent made up the entire Pack Dog Branch at Camp Rimini: Lieutenant Mace, three enlisted instructors, twenty-five trainees, and one hundred dogs.

The title "pack dog" was rather misleading, since packing was only one of the jobs the dogs could do. They could also be hitched either solo or in tandem to pull bulky loads. A pack dog could transport an average load of thirty-five pounds every day over rough terrain and could carry up to fifty pounds for limited periods. Under the supervision of a handler, loaded dogs could travel as many miles a day as the most rugged man could hike. Packing was supposed to be done when snow conditions were such that a sled or toboggan could not be used, when timber was too dense for a dog team, or when the load needing transport over snow was too small for a sled team.[7]

FIGURE 9.1. The pack dog program was started at Camp Hale, and from the beginning pack dogs were also trained to pull pulkas. (Courtesy of Lynne Mace)

A string of five or six pack dogs equipped with harness and sled or toboggan could also operate as a tandem freight team. Although strings of pack dogs did not have the speed of a standard sled dog team, they could haul bulky items that would not fit into packs.[8] Carl Lowe used a team of five Saint Bernards hitched to a basket sled to help other search and rescue sled dog teams salvage a C-54 that crashed in Newfoundland.[9]

Each pack dog was also supplied with a pulka and trained to pull a load independently. Pulkas were to be used in dense timber where a full team could not go or when the load did not justify a full sled team or even a pack dog team. A dog using a pulka could pull its own weight over rough terrain and up to three times its weight on level ground.[10]

Originally dogs were divided into two categories: either "husky" freighting teams converted to a pack string for summer work or larger dogs that could pack large loads during the summer and pull individual pulkas throughout the winter. Husky freight teams were considered a loss in the summer unless they were also trained to pack. Individual huskies could not carry as heavy a load as large packers because of their smaller build, but

FIGURE 9.2. Chesapeake Bay and Labrador retrievers were both trained for packing.
(Courtesy of Lynne Mace)

as a pack string they could carry considerable weight. During this era some people thought that using sled dogs as pack dogs ruined the team for sledding, but unless a team was used for racing, this fear proved groundless. Only sled dogs of medium (60–70 pounds) to heavy (70–110 pounds) size with a solid build were even considered for summer packing. Leggy dogs, which were more favored for racing, could not carry enough.[11]

Dog size dramatically influenced load size. It took two or three huskies to carry one man's packload, but just one of the larger dogs such as Newfoundlands, Saint Bernards, Great Pyrenees, Labradors, or Chesapeake Bay retrievers carried this same load.

Newfoundlands, which weigh about 125 pounds, could not carry as high a ratio of load to body weight as Saint Bernards or Labradors, but their good disposition, excellent fur coat, and ability to stay fit under extreme conditions all suited them for pack service. Along with Labrador and Chesapeake Bay retrievers, Saint Bernards had the highest ratio of load to body weight. Saint Bernards were of two types, short-haired and long-haired. Shorthairs were considered excellent for packing, although their coats did not suit them for use in subzero weather. The long-haired version could withstand the

FIGURE 9.3. Newfoundlands could not carry as great a ratio of load to weight as a Saint Bernard or even a Labrador, but they were considered excellent for packing. (Courtesy of Lynne Mace)

coldest weather.[12] Some Canadian Saint Bernards that had been crossbred with another unknown type of dog and were used for carting proved to be among the best dogs in the entire program. These dogs not only were huge but were incredibly tough as well. The best of all the Saint Bernards was a dog named Judge.[13] Judge did not arrive through the Dogs for Defense program as most of the pack dogs did. He used to hang around Camp Hale until one day he disrupted a review ceremony on the parade ground by howling every time the bugler blew a note. Judge was conscripted into the army and eventually found his way into the pack dog program.[14] Mace said, "If the army had had a hundred dogs like Judge, the pack dog program would have been made."[15]

Great Pyrenees were not considered exceptional pack dogs, since the available dogs had several undesirable characteristics. Many were "cowhocked" (their hind legs turned inward), which reduced their weight-carrying ability. They were also considered fussy eaters. Positive points were that they were not fighters and their coat was adequate for cold weather. They were considered to be good pack dogs if they were well selected for conformation in accordance with American Kennel Club guidelines. [16] But many of the Great Pyrenees available came from a kennel run by a politically influential woman who dumped poor-quality dogs into the Dogs for Defense program and then demanded publicity for her donations. Although the breed was used for mountain packing in Spain, most Great Pyrenees in the pack dog program had had brains as well as packing instincts bred out of them. It took six months to teach many of them only one of four most used packing commands. [17]

Chesapeake Bay retrievers were rated as having more drive and power than any other large dogs within the packing program. These dogs were of the original full-blooded strain of Chesapeakes, which were big, strong animals. Their short coats were considered a drawback, however, since it was felt they could not be used in subzero weather. [18]

In the early days of program development, Labrador retrievers were considered the best all-around pack dogs. Their coats were heavy enough to withstand cold weather, and they had a very solid build for carrying heavy loads. Only larger dogs of the breed (85–120 pounds) were supposed to be used, not smaller U.S.-bred dogs (50–65 pounds). These were the same dogs that had proved themselves along trails in the Yukon Territory as packers for white fur traders. Some larger dogs of the breed were still available in Canada. [19]

Because of inherent weaknesses in all these breeds, it eventually was determined that the entire Pack Dog Branch should be restocked with northern dogs, bred and trained solely for packing. No definite breed was considered best, but a mixture of Mackenzie River husky, malamute, wolf, and an occasional trace of Alsatian had the most of the desired qualities. Dogs were to be selected by the following criteria: weight between 110 and 135 pounds, broad heavy chests and heavy, padded shoulders, no swayback, and heavy hindquarters with straight legs. Dogs to be used for military packing were the same ones that natives in the Yukon, Alaska, and British Columbia used for packing and heavy freighting. These dogs were considered best able to withstand the rigors of the trail on little food and in extreme weather. Indian dogs were also acceptable, although their coat was not ideal. [20] Staff on buying trips bought these mongrel Indian dogs when they found them, often for trade goods instead of money. [21]

It took about three months to train a pack dog. [22] Dogs were taught to stay behind the handler instead of walking by his side in the normal "heel" position, to avoid bumping his legs or stepping on his snowshoes. "Back" was the basic command to follow the handler. Dogs were not tied to each other or put on a lead; they trailed the handler and responded to verbal commands like a sled team. The command "down," taught as a hand signal as well as a verbal command, made dogs immediately drop to the ground and was used to quickly gain their attention in the presence of any distraction or at the onset of a fight. Used along with "down" was the command "stay," which let a handler be sure that the dogs would remain where they were put as he went about other business, such as scouting the terrain or the route in military operations. The final command the dogs had to learn was "come," which brought the pack string to the handler so he did not have to return to fetch the dogs. "Come" was also used to get a lagging animal to move up. Dogs also learned this command as a hand signal. [23]

Whips were absolutely forbidden in pack dog training. Trainers used a switch on the nose, a piece of rubber hose on the hindquarters, or even the back of the hand when dogs did not respond to a simple harsh command. [24]

From the first day, dogs wore packs during all phases of training and trail work, not only to get them accustomed to the feel of them but also so they would associate the pack with getting out of the kennel for exercise. During the first week of training two burlap bags filled with straw were used to familiarize a dog with the bulk of a pack. Starting with the second week, ten-pound weights were added. Using gradual conditioning, dogs were able to pack forty-, fifty-, and then sixty-pound loads in four weeks, depending on their size. There were daily training sessions. At the outset handlers were taught not to be too affectionate when animals were being worked but to keep it businesslike. After their advanced training carrying full field loads for an entire day, dogs were run through courses with live rifle and machine-gun fire to expose them to the noises and distractions they might encounter in combat. [25]

Packs used in the program were all designed and made at the canvas shop at Camp Rimini and Fort Robinson by Edwin A. Dungan, a former saddle and harness maker. Since he had no previous experience with dog gear, his designs evolved from simple equipment used in Alaska by trappers and Eskimos and were continually being upgraded. [26] The basic design was a heavy-duty pack made of canvas with straps and buckles for closures and fittings. The double bags were fitted with a leather breast plate that helped to stabilize the load, particularly going uphill. Leather breeching around the

FIGURE 9.4. Double dog pack at Camp Rimini. (Courtesy of Greg Stevens)

hind legs prevented loads from shifting forward on the dog's neck when going downhill. Belly bands were not used like a cinch on a horse but were meant to keep the pack from swaying. Packs were originally padded with wool felt, later replaced with sheepskin. The pack also served as a harness for pulling a pulka; traces were hooked into breeching rings and shafts were fastened to the breeching straps.[27]

The pulkas used in the pack dog program had their origins with Laplanders, who used reindeer to pull them. The Swedish army developed the native pulka for use with single dogs. The U.S. Army used streamlined, tobogganlike over-snow vehicles built by Artek-Pasco, the same company that had built the sled-toboggans so hated by dog drivers. The pulkas were boatlike wooden vehicles that rode on three wooden runners shod with steel. The runners helped prevent slewing or sideslipping and also protected the wooden bottom when on hard ice. Pulkas could even float a load across water. A dog weighing 125 to 150 pounds could pull three hundred pounds on a pulka over level terrain. In mountainous terrain, the load was never to exceed a dog's weight.[28] Connectors were also improvised so that three dogs could be hitched to a pulka in tandem.[29]

Compared with sled dog teams, pack dogs never came into widespread acceptance before the war terminated. Few dogs and handlers were issued to the search and rescue units. Norman D. Vaughn, always an innovator, recognized the merits of the program, so he pushed hard for pack dogs to be assigned to the First Arctic Search and Rescue Squadron. Three pack dogs and their handler, Sgt. Hazzard H. Ruland, accompanied Vaughn to New Hampshire during the training exercise and demonstration in the White Mountains in 1944. Ruland had been a pack dog handler since the program's inception at Camp Hale in 1943. One of the dogs, named King, climbed to the summit of Mount Washington with a twenty-pound pack, perhaps the first ascent ever of this mountain by a pack dog. It was certainly the first ascent by a U.S. Army pack dog. Ruland wrote to Mace, "Vaughn was highly pleased with the pack dogs' performance, and wanted to know how huskies performed as packers."[30] Vaughn, too, was seeking a multipurpose animal. His comments helped initiate the program for breeding northern dogs to wolves.

The wolf hybrid program envisioned at Camp Rimini was just starting to produce pups at Fort Robinson at the war's end. If it had continued, it might have created a perfect military transport dog. There is no doubt that a large, rugged northern type of dog capable of pulling heavily loaded sleds in winter and packing large loads in the summer would ultimately have been bred. This would have answered both military needs with the same animal, a philosophy strongly favored by the military hierarchy. In fact, the change from large-breed dogs to northern crossbreeds that was occurring in late 1944 was the first step in the integration of sled dogs and pack dogs, which would have brought the program full circle.

10. Sled Dogs and the SS

German Dog Teams of World War II

In the forests of Finland during World War II, German mountain divisions fought side by side with their Finnish allies against both Russian soldiers and the relentless frozen desolation of this hinterland. Movement across terrain covered with deep snow was limited at best, and skis were the best method. Most supplies were moved by draft animals pulling sleighs. Both reindeer and military sled dog teams were harnessed for this use.

These dog teams were part of the Field Dog Echelon of the German Sixth ss Mountain Division (NORD), the only German military unit that had sled dogs as part of its official organization. This unit was assembled in 1943 from the area around Berlin and sent to join seasoned veterans in Finland. (Many troops serving in combat or *Waffen* ss units were drafted and assigned to these organizations. They did not volunteer.) The canine section comprised three distinct dog groups: scout dogs, messenger dogs, and sled dogs, or *Ziehhunden*. The sled dog group was originally viewed with great skepticism. Thirty men were assigned to the division's canine section, but only four were designated *Hundeführer*, or dog driver—the equivalent of a musher. This unit used sled techniques influenced by the Finns, who had successfully used military dog teams during their "Winter War" with the Soviet Union. The Field Dog Echelon was used primarily to haul supplies and evacuate the wounded, serving both in Finland and in the Vosges Mountains of France.[1]

Sixteen dogs were originally assigned to the German sled dog section that served loyally throughout the northern campaign. Dogs were classified as mixed breeds, even though the German *Ski Training and Tactics Manual* of 1942 recommended either Eskimo, Newfoundland, Siberian, or Lapland dogs for pulling sleds. Traits of these breeds were the primary selection criteria. Most people who encountered these animals described them as

FIGURE 10.1. Finnish soldiers hook up a pulka team during the "Winter War" with the Soviet Union. (Author's collection)

wolflike in both appearance and behavior,[2] the way the uneducated tend to describe any sled dog. It took approximately two months to train German dogs for sled duty, with the smartest being used as lead dogs.[3]

Typically, dogs were harnessed in a three-dog tandem hitch using a leather chest harness instead of the old "horse collar" harness that the Americans and the Finns used for a tandem hitch at that time. The teams were hitched between wooden shafts as for pulling a pulka. Dogs could also be harnessed in a fan hitch, with tuglines, or traces, attached to the back of their harnesses,[4] but because of the densely forested terrain, the tandem hitch was primarily used. The sled itself was a Finnish *akja*, a boatlike wooden sled. The *akja* was approximately six feet long and twenty-two inches wide—the general width of a military ski column track. It was similar to the sled that German ski troops hauled by hand.[5] Drivers did not ride *akjas*; during the winter they used skis, and on favorable terrain they often skijored (were towed by a rope attached to the dogs). In deep snow and difficult terrain drivers would help their teams pull the sleds. During the limited summer, axles and eighteen-inch wheels were bolted to the *akjas*, and drivers walked alongside their teams. Teams were directed in the same manner as in most

FIGURE 10.2. Dog team from the field dog section of the Sixth German SS
Mountain Division in Finland. This is the only known photo of this specialized
unit. (Courtesy of Otto Schulz. Photo computer enhanced by Mike Jones)

dog sled operations, by voice command only. Commands were *Hussa!* for go,
Halt! for stop, *Links!* for left, and *Rechts!* for right—the same basic signals
used universally, except for the language difference.[6]

Sled teams transported ammunition and supplies to front-line units fighting a trench-style stalemate war. Troops on both sides of the conflict were
living in primitive bunkers, with attacks and counterattacks resulting in
brutal hand-to-hand combat. Those wounded, as well as those with frost-
bite, hypothermia, and such, were evacuated to the rear by the dog teams
that brought ammunition. Teams were also sent forward of positions under
fire to recover the wounded. On one of these missions, two out of three
dogs were wounded, and the *akja* was heavily damaged by fire from enemy
automatic weapons. There is no known official record of the total number of
soldiers evacuated by dogs, but the diary of Otto Schulz, the only surviving
dog driver, records that his team transported 354 wounded soldiers (both
German and Soviets) from the front lines to medical facilities during the
battles in the Karelian area. Wounded dogs also were evacuated and treated.

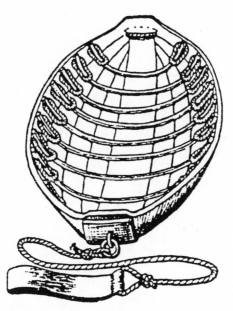

FIGURE 10.3. Finnish *akja*, a boatlike wooden sled used by ski troops. (Sketch from War Department, Military Intelligence Division, *German Winter Warfare*)

All dogs that died were buried with full military honors. They were later replaced by dogs from a police unit and by captured Russian dogs.[7]

Although German mushers were used as over-snow ambulance drivers, their only medical training was a briefing on loosening tourniquets while en route to help reduce limb loss. Because Soviet soldiers did not necessarily honor the Geneva Accords, which stated that medical personnel were noncombatants and were not to be fired on if they displayed a red cross, while they were in Finland all drivers were armed. They were issued the Mauser K-98, the short bolt-action rifle used by most German mountain troopers. But their weapon of choice whenever possible was a captured Russian PPsh-41 machine pistol.[8] It was compact, extremely reliable in harsh conditions, and had plenty of firepower with a seventy-one-round drum magazine.

The German division, including its sled dog section, was eventually withdrawn from the northern area of operations and sent to the Western Front for "Operation Nordwind" in support of the faltering Ardennes campaign

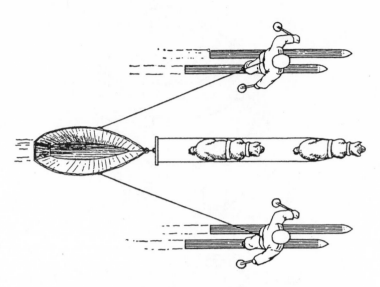

FIGURE 10.4. The drivers helped the dogs pull in difficult terrain. (Sketch from War Department, Military Intelligence Division, *German Winter Warfare*)

(the Battle of the Bulge). This German division moved over 1,800 miles,[9] but by this time there were only seven dogs left in the entire section.[10]

In the Vosges Mountains of France dog teams continued to operate as they had in Finland, transporting supplies and ammunition and evacuating the wounded. It was in this same area during World War I that the French mountain troops had used sled dog teams for the same purpose. Otto Schulz's diary noted that his dogs evacuated 120 wounded men, including some American soldiers, during this phase of the unit's history. One of his accounts describes the team's being spotted by an Allied aircraft on patrol while evacuating a wounded soldier. "The plane had us out in the open and had begun its strafing run when I pulled out a flag marked with a red cross. I stood there at the head of my team, clutching my flag while praying that it could be seen, and held my ground. On seeing my flag, the pilot honored it and held his fire, allowing us to proceed on our way without incident."[11]

During the Battle of the Bulge, at Maj. Norman D. Vaughn's suggestion, the U.S. Army attempted to gather dog sled teams from Arctic search and rescue units to evacuate the wounded in this same area. During operational planning U.S. dog drivers, whose teams normally consisted of nine dogs to a sled, decided to use only four dogs per team to transport the wounded, similar to the German technique. They thought it would attract less attention than dashing in like cavalry troops. This technique would also make better use of the dogs, since loads would be much lighter than those normally pulled by nine dogs. But by the time the U.S. dog teams were assembled, the snow had melted and turned to mud. They were useless for their mission and were sent back to their home bases.[12]

After this campaign in the Vosges Mountains, the Sixth ss Mountain Division (NORD), along with remnants of its canine unit, fought a rear-guard mission, finally capitulating to U.S. forces in Bavaria during the closing days of the war.[13] With its surrender, the Nordic-style dog-mushing unit with a very small but unique military mission faded into oblivion.

Like the sled dogs used on failed polar explorations, none of the division's sled dogs survived their journey home. The last dog was run over by a tank during the final days of the war.[14] Many soldiers of this division owed their survival to the dogs, and a memorial to fallen four-legged comrades has been dedicated in Austria.

*

11. Dog Team Déjà Vu

Big Delta, Alaska

During the aftermath of World War II, as U.S. military forces were still scaling back, a new threat appeared: the cold war. Intense economic, political, and military rivalry between the United States and the Soviet Union began in earnest. This significant era lasted for fifty years, dictating the foremost mission of U.S. Army preparedness for possible conflict. Analysis of U.S. operations during World War II showed considerable deficiency in cold-weather military operations, particularly in the army.[1] The prospect of combat with the Soviet Union underscored dramatically that 65 percent of the Eurasian landmass lies in Arctic and subarctic latitudes.[2] Recognizing a weak link in U.S. forces' capabilities, Pentagon officials acted. By 1948 the roots of the cold war were firmly established. Facing the real possibility of fighting a war in bitter cold, they established the Arctic Indoctrination School at Big Delta, Alaska.

The core curriculum at the new school included military mountaineering, skiing, and Arctic survival techniques. The terrain around Big Delta boasted glaciers, mountains, tundra, and rivers, and with some of the coldest recorded temperatures in North America, it was considered an ideal training ground. Most of the hands-on instruction was conducted in the field, far from any normal logistical support. Since snowmobiles were not yet common even in the military, the army decided to use the traditional Alaskan over-snow transportation system: dog teams. After all, reasoned elite planners, the army had amassed years of experience with dog teams during World War II. At some point the top brass realized that these army assets had long since been transferred to the U.S. Air Force, but the decision had been made. In typical military fashion, they created a "big picture," and someone else far down the chain of command had to fill in the details to make it work.

Sgt. Jesse Taylor and Cpl. C. A. "Charlie" Boyd were assigned the task of building a dog kennel and starting a sled dog operation near an old air base at Big Delta. These two men made up the entire dog section at this newly formed Arctic school. As it happens, the Big Delta airfield had been used by Soviet pilots flying Lend-Lease aircraft from Alaska to Siberia during World War II.[3] Rescue of pilots who crashed along this route had been the reason dog teams were used in Arctic regions during World War II. It was fitting that the new Arctic Indoctrination School was established on a site loaded with historical precedent. As with its sled dog program early in Tenth Mountain Division history, the army was starting at square one. Despite four years of intense and innovative experience with sled dogs in its recent past, the army was reinventing the wheel. The men assigned to start the program had almost no experience with sled dogs. At least Taylor had worked with animals as a boy in West Virginia. His father had used horses in a timber cutting operation, and Taylor had learned the basics of team driving from him. Like most people from the Appalachians, Taylor had owned dogs as well.[4] Boyd had worked a little with an Indian dog team and driver contracted to support an army operation at his previous assignment at Lake Louise in Canada.[5]

One primary difference between this déjà vu with dog teams and army history was that Sergeant Taylor had at least been issued a copy of *FM 25-6*, the army field manual on dog transportation. With this bible in hand, his first step was acquiring dogs and equipment. Since no dogs were available locally, he procured them from all over the country. Dogs were imported from New England as well as from the U.S. Air Force Survival School at Nome, since the air force had not yet totally phased out dog teams from its search and rescue inventory. He even found two dogs that had a history of Antarctic service. Eventually the kennel held sixty dogs.[6] This total was later reduced to only twenty by direction of the school commandant. Someone decided they should maintain only enough dogs for two complete nine-dog teams plus a couple of females for breeding.[7]

Because Sergeant Taylor was operating independently, without any sled dog experience, he readily experimented with new ideas of his own. He was not satisfied with the standard dog harness, so he adapted a local version. It was made of cotton webbing like a standard military harness, but was designed more like older types that used a breast strap. Taylor had seen that frozen harnesses would chafe dogs' flanks. In his version the side straps rode

FIGURE II.I. The dog kennel at Big Delta eventually held sixty dogs. This total was later reduced to only enough dogs for two teams plus two females for continued breeding. (Courtesy of Judy Ferguson)

higher on the dogs' backs than in the military low back draft harness, so they had very little contact with snow and required little thawing out after use.[8]

A sled-building facility no longer existed anywhere in the army. All the sled-building experience that had produced excellent military sled models during World War II had long since been forgotten. Information about sled construction had apparently been misplaced or discarded after the war. Sergeant Taylor obtained a fifteen-foot Greenland "Big Bertha" sled for use at the Arctic Indoctrination School, no doubt a castoff from an air force unit in the area. This particular sled was constructed using ax handles for stanchions. Taylor later said that the sled was extremely heavy and had been built by German prisoners of war during World War II,[9] meaning it had been constructed at Fort Robinson, Nebraska. This "Big Bertha" sled was used in conjunction with the army "ahkio" (*akja*) to haul up to 2,400 pounds of gear supporting the men training at the school.[10]

Students were divided into four-man tent groups, which would each haul all its basic winter survival equipment, including tent, Yukon stove, fuel, and rations, in a fiberglass version of the Finnish *akja*. The original Finnish snow

FIGURE II.2. Not being satisfied with the standard military dog harness, Sgt. Jesse Taylor adapted a "retro" harness from a local design. (Courtesy of Judy Ferguson)

boat was wooden, often with a copper-clad bottom, and pulled by reindeer. The U.S. Army version was made of fiberglass with a canvas cover. Its official designation was "Sled, Scow-Type, 200-Pound Capacity (Ahkio)." It was eighty-eight inches long, twenty-four inches wide, and eight inches deep. Normally the men towed it themselves, either on skis or on snowshoes, wearing harnesses and traces as early polar explorers did. [11] Sergeant Taylor connected a string of a dozen ahkios to the rear of his sled, spaced about five inches apart. He said that the trick to keeping the ahkios from turning over was to always keep the connecting ropes taut. With this train of sleds, a team of nine dogs could carry a much greater load than with just one basic sled. [12] This fact had been discovered long ago by military dog drivers, but trailer sleds were just not available to Sergeant Taylor at the time. Taylor also experimented with hitching a single dog to one ahkio, equivalent to a pack dog with a pulka. [13]

In 1949 the Argentine army asked the U.S. Army for help in training and equipping members of its armed forces in dog team operations. These dogs and troops were designated to support Argentine scientific bases in Antarctica before dog team use was banned by international treaties concerned with possible contamination of the unique Antarctic continent. The Argentine army had never used sled dogs in its normal forces, despite the country's topography and its closeness to southern polar regions.[14] Because they were the army sled dog experts, the men at the Arctic Indoctrination School were assigned to provide training and equipment to this group of foreign soldiers. A paramount assignment was locating suitable dogs. Charlie Boyd was sent all over Alaska to acquire dogs. In Nome, he found a large black-and-white dog pulling an Eskimo boy around. This dog, named Mike, allegedly was the sole survivor of a hunting party that had perished on the ice in the Bering Strait. Boyd bought Mike, who became his lead dog.[15] They even rounded up strays to obtain the fifty dogs required for Argentina.[16] Taylor considered Lab–Siberian husky mixes best for sled dogs because they had more spirit and made superior freighting teams. These Labradors were the larger-bodied variety still found in the North and favored by Indians. Taylor trained an entire litter of pups from his best dogs as leaders. When they were out in the field the dogs were fed dried fish, as was the native custom.[17]

Two major functions of the dog section were hauling supplies to troops during field training exercises and evacuating the injured. As was common in ski training and field exercises in the Tenth Mountain Division during early years of World War II, soldiers injured by cold and other trauma had to be brought out to major road networks or to frozen lakes where a Norseman aircraft could land. Dogs were used for this again at Big Delta. When the Korean War broke out in 1950 and the cold war became a hot war in a cold climate, Sergeant Taylor advocated using dogs to evacuate wounded soldiers from the battleground. He believed that dogs, with their lower profiles, would be a safer mode of transportation in evacuations.[18] As in the previous war, this technique was never seriously considered for combat. Helicopters were battle tested during the Korean War and proved to be the most efficient battlefield ambulances.

Sergeant Taylor had to provide much of the dogs' medical care himself. Like his predecessors in other times and places, he became adept at suturing injured animals in the field. He carried several kits consisting of a sterilized suture needle and thread prepared by the hospital for such emergencies. In one particular incident Taylor put forty stitches in a dog after a dog fight, not knowing whether the dog would survive. Six weeks later the dog was back in harness.[19]

Another accident did not turn out so well. Taylor drove his team off a hidden twenty-five-foot cliff. The sled, with Taylor still hanging on to it, landed on one of his wheel dogs (dogs positioned directly in front of the sled). The dog seemed unharmed and continued to work. But several days later the dog's intestine ruptured and it died. Traveling down Black Rapids Glacier, Taylor was driving a sled with a soldier skijoring behind when an unseen snow bridge began to collapse. All of them miraculously made it to the other side before the crevasse totally opened up beneath them.[20]

Sled dogs and drivers were used at the Arctic school for only about six years (1948–54).[21] Lessons learned during the Korean War confirmed the army's need for a cold-weather school, which continues today as the Northern Warfare Training Center at Fort Greely, Alaska. Helicopters finally replaced sled dogs in the army, just as they had in the air force. Helicopters proved their value in Korea not only as ambulances but as supply vehicles. This second era of dog teams within the army lasted longer than the major program during World War II. But there were no technical advances or other real innovations, since the few participants had none of the expertise or support that had been available to drivers at Camp Hale, Colorado, Camp Rimini, Montana, or Fort Robinson, Nebraska. Working alone, they had to relearn forgotten lessons of the past. Like many soldiers of the cold war, they simply did their duty to the best of their ability without fanfare. Now almost all traces of their service have disappeared.

12. Sled Dogs and Secret Surveillance

Sledge Patrol SIRIUS

The only military operation in the world that still uses sled dogs is the Danish Sledge Patrol SIRIUS. Its beginnings can be traced to the early years of World War II, when a group of civilian Danish and Norwegian trappers and hunters, along with a few Eskimos, formed a volunteer sled patrol to provide surveillance in remote areas of Greenland and try to prevent Germans from establishing weather stations there. Since weather patterns that developed over Greenland would greatly influence European weather several days later, Greenland was of significant strategic importance to both the Allies and the Axis powers. In the fall of 1941, Admiral (then Captain) Edward "Iceberg" Smith of the U.S. Coast Guard and Eske Brun, the Danish governor of Greenland, agreed that the Sledge Patrol would work for the U.S. Army.[1] This fifteen-man organization commanded by Ib Poulsen forced German weather teams to continually relocate to avoid capture.

The patrol's original mission was to perform regular surveillance and reconnaissance along the coast of Greenland as far north as seventy-seven degrees latitude. It was recognized that local trappers on the patrol had knowledge of the area that could not be duplicated, and that the territory was so vast that every means available was needed to adequately report signs of enemy occupancy. Members of the patrol used native *komatik* sleds with dogs harnessed in a typical fan hitch. All patrol affiliates were armed with their own hunting rifles. When the Germans located one of the patrol's huts and found soft-nosed rifle ammunition, they left a note accusing the patrol of violating the Geneva Conventions forbidding the use of soft lead bullets, or "dumdums."[2]

Playing a deadly game of hide-and-seek, sledge men prowled the desolate region for two months at a time. The patrol was very successful: of five

German landing attempts during the war, the Sledge Patrol discovered three. Aerial surveillance was not particularly successful, since German forces could see aircraft from the ground whereas their own movement was not detected from the air.[3] During one encounter with Germans, a member of the patrol, Eli Knudsen, was shot and killed right on his sled. The patrol inadvertently supplied dog team transportation to the Germans, who captured five teams and used them for their operations. As Germans abandoned their outpost on Sabine Island, which had been discovered and attacked by U.S. forces, they killed two captured teams while they were still in their harnesses.[4] Their killing these teams demonstrates how valuable they were considered as implements of war in the hostile environment of Greenland. The loosely formed wartime Sledge Patrol was disbanded at the end of World War II.

In deepest secrecy, the sledge patrol was renewed in 1950 during the cold war. It was reestablished as a result of the judgment of the World Court at The Hague in 1933, which deliberated Norway's and Denmark's claims to sovereignty in Greenland and awarded the area to Denmark. A ground mobile unit was chosen to fulfill sovereignty requirements based on topography, weather, and experience gained during the war, since aerial surveillance had proved less than adequate. This task of maintaining Danish sovereignty in uninhabited portions of Greenland fell to the Naval Command and was accomplished using dogsleds. The mission's code name was Operation RESO-LUT. This secret mission became public knowledge in 1953, and the name was changed to the Sledge Patrol SIRIUS.[5] This name, which the Danes always write in capitals,[6] derived from Sirius, the dog star, the brightest star in the constellation Canis Major, the "big dog." It indicates just how important the sled dog is to the success of this strategic operation.

The SIRIUS patrol is responsible for an uninhabited region the size of England and France combined, almost 62,000 square miles. This area, known as North and Northeast Greenland, makes up Greenland National Park. It is a high Arctic environment with temperatures reaching as low as minus fifty-eight degrees Fahrenheit and with wind speeds gusting to more than one hundred knots at times. Since the sun stays below the horizon between three to four and a half months out of the year, lack of light makes it hard to move around. Even in the twenty-first century, weather and topography still make movement during winter almost impossible by any means other than dogsled. The Sledge Patrol SIRIUS covers more than 12,000 miles annually by dogsled, and since its establishment it has traversed over 341,000 miles.[7]

FIGURE 12.1. Sledge Patrol SIRIUS team beginning its spring travels with a heavily loaded sled. (Courtesy of Poul Ipsen)

The patrol consists of six teams of two men each. Patrol members are volunteers from all three Danish services (army, navy, and air force); each must hold at least the rank of sergeant and have an exceptional service record. After passing strenuous physical and psychological tests, they are given additional training to prepare them for their military mission in Greenland, including winter combat and survival techniques, medicine, communications, and engine mechanics. Since there are no service or support personnel in any patrol territory, the twelve team members must have thorough knowledge of all necessary survival skills. Assignment is for a tour of twenty-six months with no leave or other time off, since the Greenland patrol operates twenty-four hours a day, seven days a week. Rank and military specialty are dispensed with during this tour; everyone must cook, clean, maintain equipment, train dogs, and actively patrol. Maximum individual effort is required to complete missions under the severe conditions of this remote outpost.[8]

New patrol members arrive during the summer and are teamed with another person who has already completed the first year of the tour. Thus each sled team is assigned a "new" and an "old" patroller for the upcoming winter. During this short period of summer teams must go out and cache supplies for their patrols during the following winter, as well as perform any

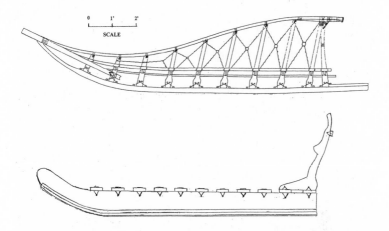

FIGURE 12.2. World War II U.S. Greenland sled "Big Bertha" compared with the contemporary sled used by Sledge Patrol SIRIUS. (Illustration by author)

necessary maintenance on huts and supply depots.[9] During these warmer, lighter months, surveillance is conducted by boat and aircraft.[10]

Beginning in September, patrollers build their own dogsleds and other equipment. They also begin to seriously train their dogs. Except for a few minor changes, their sleds are the same as those used by the native Eskimo population since the beginning of dogsledding—a *komatik* type, approximately thirteen feet long by thirty-six inches wide and constructed of ash and plywood. Today plastic shoes are added to the runners, having recently replaced the old iron shoes. The new material is currently being tested with very successful results and reduces overall sled weight by almost forty pounds. This extremely strong sled is ideal for use on hard ice. SIRIUS patrol members build their own sleds to give them a thorough understanding of construction in case repairs are needed on the trail, the way U.S. dog drivers in World War II helped in sled construction. Instead of traditional animal sinew or rawhide, the sled is lashed together with four-millimeter nylon cord, which is stronger, easier to use, and easier to obtain than sinew.[11]

The men also make the dog harnesses using nylon webbing; they are similar in design to traditional lightweight racing harnesses, with felt padding. In the future these are to be replaced by premade harnesses padded with neoprene, similar to an X-back racing harness. Dogs are hitched either in a traditional fan configuration or in a paired gang hitch that the Danes know as a Nome hitch. In extremely soft snow, dogs are hitched in true tandem fashion, one behind the other. [12]

Dogs are all bred from Greenlander dogs originally from Disko Bay, later supplemented by dogs from Thule and Scoresbysund. Breeding is done entirely by the sledge men. The result has been a larger and heavier stock dog more capable of pulling heavy loads for the extended time on patrol. A whip is still used in the traditional way as an aid to training, particularly since there are no typical trails on which to learn directions. The whip is snapped on the side opposite the way the dogs are to move, in conjunction with a voice command. In moving away from the whip crack, one dog pushes others over. [13]

As winter approaches each year, the men decide the priority of each sled team for claiming new puppies, affectionately called *vappers*. There is a christening party at which dogs are named, governed by strict traditions guarded by the kennel masters. Names are chosen by the sled team members who will drive the dogs. Although dogs are not at the ceremony, the drivers make a speech about each puppy, revealing the dog's name. Since the patrollers toast every new name with some type of strong drink, it is a time of great revelry, christening twenty to twenty-five pups. [14] The importance of dogs to the team is evident in this celebration, since the only other organized event that gives relief from daily responsibilities is Christmas dinner.

In November, when the ice is strong enough to support them, teams begin their sled patrols. Five teams, each consisting of two men and eleven dogs, fan out from headquarters at Daneborg to cover patrol routes. Two patrol members remain behind to operate the radios required to communicate with each team. [15] Sleds are heavily loaded with the equipment and supplies dictated by the harsh environment. The sled carries ten gallons of fuel for a Primus stove, food for the dogs as well as the men, radio, tents, sleeping bags, and other mission essentials such as cameras, binoculars, clothing, and extra batteries. Sleeping bags are designed with an inner and an outer bag. The outer bag is made of flame-resistant Nomex and is large enough for two persons in an emergency. The inner bag is also large enough to allow freedom of movement while wearing extra clothes. The bags are used with insulated sleeping mats. Each cylindrical tent is of specially made cotton fabric and can withstand extremely strong winds. [16] Dogs, like sled dogs everywhere, are staked out in the elements. Sleds are so heavily loaded with essential survival and mission equipment that drivers do not ride on them but wear skis. One man may even ski in front of the sled, breaking trail and finding the route, while the other skis beside the sled, helping the dogs when necessary. Patroller Poul Ibsen said, "Thank God that the old wooden NATO skis [are] being replaced with modern fiberglass ones."[17]

The Sledge Patrol SIRIUS is a military operation, and men are armed while on patrol. Weapons are primarily for self-defense against animals such as polar bears or for hunting. Injury or death of any dogs in a bear encounter could be catastrophic to the entire team. The last time a patrol had to kill a polar bear was in the late 1980s. Firearms can also be used to put down an injured dog if necessary. The weapon each sledge man carries is an old U.S. M1917 Enfield .30–06-caliber rifle, also known as the Eddystone rifle. This bolt-action rifle is quite simple, considered very reliable under extreme Arctic conditions, and more than adequate firepower, since the patrol's mission is surveillance and reconnaissance instead of combat. The men carry both soft-nose hunting bullets and full metal jacket military ammunition.[18]

In addition to its military surveillance, the patrol represents civilian authority in the area, like the old Northwest Mounted Police, and team members are armed for this task as well. Each carries a ten-millimeter Glock 20 semiautomatic pistol for self-defense. It too uses both hollow-point and military ball ammunition.[19] The police function used to be enforcing hunting regulations, but today the patrols' primary policing involves monitoring scientific and other expeditions within the national park.[20] They also report on animal life in the district.[21]

Teams travel approximately six hundred to eight hundred miles in the fall, returning to base by Christmas. They cover a daily distance of twenty-two miles in an average of four to eight hours, but if storms hinder progress they may make only three miles or less in a day. In addition to travel time, each day consists of setting up and breaking camp, feeding and caring for the dogs, repairing equipment, communication, and preparing food.[22]

Teams depart again on patrol in February. These "spring travels" last up to four and a half months. Some teams are flown to the extreme boundaries of the territory and must then make the trip back to base, arriving in mid-June. By this time the men and dogs will have covered 1,500 to 2,000 miles. Most of the time they do not encounter another human being. The incredible vastness of the area traversed for hours on end is punctuated only by the

FIGURE 12.3. The age-old sound of singing dogs will continue in the new millennium with the Sledge Patrol SIRIUS. (Courtesy of Poul Ipsen)

northern lights and occasional sightings of polar bears or Arctic wolves. Former sledge man Peter Mikkelsen recalls that "it gives you the ultimate feeling of freedom."[23]

Although it may seem that dogsleds are an obsolete mode of transportation in this age of space travel, it has been continually proved that under the conditions of geography and climate existing in polar Greenland, sled dogs are still far superior to aircraft and tracked vehicles. A dog requires no repair shops or spare parts. The Sledge Patrol SIRIUS still operates as efficiently and economically as it has for almost fifty years. The sled dog is so essential to the success of the SIRIUS mission that it is in the center of the unit's crest, which is worn in Denmark only by sledge men who have completed a full twenty-six months on the patrol.[24] It represents the accomplishment of traveling 2,500 to 4,400 miles with only their dogs for company, an experience they will never forget. In one of the most desolate and inhospitable regions on earth, the dog is still man's best friend.

The Sledge Patrol SIRIUS continues alone in the modern world as a living tribute to all those men and dogs who have served on the far frozen frontiers of their empires.

Epilogue

A serious tragedy struck the Sledge Patrol SIRIUS in mid-October 1999. Radio contact was lost with the station at Mestersvig, and a helicopter sent to investigate found the station deserted. The two people normally stationed there had disappeared, along with a sled and all the dogs except one. A search team dispatched to Mestersvig followed all the sled tracks found in the area and ultimately discovered the men and dogs dead under the ice of Noret inlet, only two miles from the station. The men had apparently taken their sled team for a conditioning run along the inlet shore. These dogs were reserves for the SIRIUS sledge teams, and the duties at Mestersvig included ensuring that they were kept in excellent physical condition. For some reason the dogs veered onto thin ice, causing the sledge to break through. Poul Ipsen of SIRIUS lamented: "None of us can understand what made the dogs run out on the ice. They were all old and very experienced dogs that normally have a very good feeling about the ice conditions and therefore avoid thin ice. The answer does not matter much now. It will not bring us our friends back." The two men died in a valiant effort to free the dogs from their tuglines. Even in the grip of death, the bond between men and sled dogs in the Arctic is paramount.

This tragedy is the second loss of human life the patrol has suffered in its fifty years of operation. Dan L. H. Laursen and Martin Højsgaard Hansen, along with their ten dogs, are the last casualties of almost a hundred years of military dog mushing in the twentieth century. The loss demonstrates the dangers and hardships encountered every day by the men and dogs who gallantly soldiered for their countries in the cold and snow of distant dominions. Let us not forget their tracks in the snow.

Notes

I. SLED DOGS SUPPLY SOLDIERS

1. Jerry Ray Nelson, "Blazer of Trails," *Mushing* 67 (March–April 1999): 21–22.
2. Nelson, "Blazer of Trails."
3. Nelson, "Blazer of Trails."
4. Dominique Cellura, *Travelers of the Cold: Sled Dogs of the Far North* (Anchorage: Alaska Northwest Books, 1989), 14–15.
5. Nelson, "Blazer of Trails."
6. Nelson, "Blazer of Trails."
7. Nelson, "Blazer of Trails," 23.
8. Nelson, "Blazer of Trails," 24.
9. Cellura, *Travelers of the Cold*, 32.
10. Barry Gregory, *Mountain and Arctic Warfare: From Alexander to Afghanistan* (Wellingborough, Eng.: Patrick Stephens, 1989), 30.
11. Shannon Garst, *Scotty Allan, King of the Dog Team Drivers* (New York: Julian Messner, 1946), 202.
12. Garst, *Scotty Allan*, 204–6.
13. Garst, *Scotty Allan*, 207–12.
14. Garst, *Scotty Allan*, 214–16.
15. France, Ministère de la Défense, "Tot Dret," *Bulletin d'Information de l'École Militaire de Haute Montagne* (Chamonix), n.d., 16.
16. France, Ministère de la Défense, "Tot Dret."
17. Gregory, *Mountain and Arctic Warfare*, 50.
18. Luciano Viazzi, "Guerra 1915–18: Sull'Adamello i cani da traino," *Alpino*, 1986, 26.
19. Viazzi, "Guerra 1915–18," 27–28.
20. Viazzi, "Guerra 1915–18," 29.
21. Viazzi, "Guerra 1915–18."
22. Viazzi, "Guerra 1915–18."
23. Viazzi, "Guerra 1915–18."
24. *R.A.S.C. (Royal Army Service Corps) Quarterly* (London) 14, no. 2 (April 1926): 53–54.

25. *R.A.S.C. (Royal Army Service Corps) Training, Animal Transport, Part III* (London: War Office, 1922), 3.
26. War Department, *Technical Regulation No. 1380-20, Dog Transportation* (Washington DC: War Department, June 15, 1926), 1.
27. War Department, *TR. No. 1380–20*, 7.
28. War Department, *FM 25–6, Dog Transportation* (Washington DC: War Department, August 19, 1944), 72.
29. War Department, *TR. No. 1380–20*, 2.
30. War Department, *TR. No. 1380–20*, 2–3.
31. Ministère de la Défense, "Tot Dret."
32. Michael G. Lemish, *War Dogs: Canines in Combat* (Washington DC: Brassey's, 1996), 64.

2. SLED DOGS ENTER THE SERVICE

1. "New England Sled Dog Club History," fiftieth anniversary club booklet (1974), printed from the Internet June 1999 (www.gsinet.net/~black/history.htm).
2. Joan McDonald Brearley, *This Is the Siberian Husky* (Neptune City NJ, T.F.S., 1974), 119.
3. "New England Sled Dog Club History."
4. "New England Sled Dog Club History."
5. "New England Sled Dog Club History."
6. Brearley, *Siberian Husky*, 102–22.
7. David W. Armstrong Jr., "World War II Memoirs" (unpublished), Helena MT, June 1977, 1.
8. Armstrong memoirs.
9. War Department, *Table of Organization and Equipment, No. 1–618, Army Air Forces, Arctic Search and Rescue Squadron, Flight Control Command* (Washington DC: War Department, September 15, 1943), 15.
10. War Department, *FM 25–6, Dog Transportation* (Washington DC: War Department, August 19, 1944), 22.
11. David W. Armstrong Jr., letter to author, April 15, 1997.
12. Stuart A. Mace, interview and transcript by Karen Fischer, Ashcroft CO, January 1982, S1/9.
13. Armstrong memoirs, 4.
14. Armstrong memoirs, 4.
15. Armstrong memoirs, 4.
16. Richard S. Moulton, telephone interview with author, May 1999.
17. Armstrong memoirs, 5.

18. Armstrong memoirs, 5.
19. Armstrong memoirs, 96.

3. SLED DOGS AND SKI TROOPS

1. Stuart A. Mace, interview and transcript by Karen Fischer, Ashcroft CO, January 1982, S1/1–4.
2. Mace interview, S1/8.
3. Mace interview, S1/6.
4. Mace interview, S1/9.
5. Mace interview, S1/6.
6. Stuart A. Mace, "Recollections of Stuart A. Mace, about His Army Service, the Tenth Mountain Division, and Military Dog Sledding," video interview by W. Michael Meyers, Snowmass CO, August 10, 1991.
7. Mace interview, S1/7.
8. Army Ground Forces, *History of the Mountain Training Center* (N.p., n.d.), Denver Public Library, Western History Department, 99.
9. Mace interview, S1/10.
10. Mace interview, S1/10.
11. Mace interview, S1/10.
12. Army Ground Forces, *History of the Mountain Training Center.*
13. Mace, "Recollections."
14. Mace interview, S2/1.
15. Mace interview, S1/12.
16. Mace interview, S1/2.
17. Mountain and Winter Warfare Board, Camp Hale CO, Letter and endorsements, To: Headquarters and Services Supply, Washington DC, March 5, 1943, Development Project, Sledge, Dog, 5th Ind.
18. Mace interview, S2/1.
19. Mountain and Winter Warfare Board, letter and endorsements, 1st Ind.
20. Mountain and Winter Warfare Board, letter and endorsements, 3rd Ind.
21. Mountain and Winter Warfare Board, letter and endorsements, 5th Ind.
22. Mace interview, S1/5.
23. Mace, "Recollections."
24. Mountain and Winter Warfare Board, Mountain Training Center, Camp Hale CO, report, May 10, 1943, To: Capt. Richard Leonard, Office of the Quartermaster General, Washington DC, 2.
25. Mace interview, S4/3.
26. Mace interview, S1/9.
27. Mountain and Winter Warfare Board, letter and endorsements, 11th Ind.
28. Army Ground Forces, *History of the Mountain Training Center.*

29. Army Ground Forces, *History of the Mountain Training Center,* 15.
30. Mace interview, S2/2.

4. SLED DOG CENTER

1. Karen Fischer, "Training Sled Dogs at Camp Rimini, 1942–1944," *Montana, the Magazine of Western History* (Montana Historical Society, Helena) 34 (Winter 1984): 11.
2. Fischer, "Training Sled Dogs," 10.
3. Stuart A. Mace, interview and transcript by Karen Fischer, Ashcroft CO, January 1982, S2/4.
4. Mace interview, S2/4.
5. "Training Dogs for War," *Mountain Bell Magazine,* 1942, 4.
6. Mace interview, S2/5.
7. David W. Armstrong Jr., "World War II Memoirs" (unpublished), Helena MT, June 1997, 1.
8. Mace interview, S2/6.
9. Armstrong memoirs, 5.
10. Mace interview, S3/10.
11. "A lifetime with Dogs: Eddie Barbeau," *Montana Sled Dog Newsletter* (Helena) 4, no. 3 (Winter 1992): 1–2.
12. Armstrong memoirs, 17.
13. Mace interview, S5/1.
14. Mace interview, S6/3.
15. Mace interview, S8/2.
16. Mace interview, S2/4.
17. Fischer, "Training Sled Dogs," 16.
18. Mace interview, S8/9.
19. Fischer, "Training Sled Dogs," 16–17.
20. Mace interview, S8/10–11.
21. Mace interview, S8/1–2.
22. Armstrong memoirs, 17.
23. Mace interview, S3/9.
24. Armstrong memoirs, 24.
25. Mace interview, S4/9.
26. Armstrong memoirs, 13.
27. Mace interview, S4/8.
28. Mace interview, S7/8.
29. Mace interview, S4/6–7.
30. Mace interview, S4/6–7.
31. Mace interview, S2/9.

32. Mace interview, S1/9.
33. Mace interview, S2/9.
34. John A. Matovich, telephone interview with the author, November 26, 1996.
35. Mace interview, S3/6.
36. Mace interview, S9/4.
37. Armstrong memoirs, 13.
38. Fischer, "Training Sled Dogs."

5. SLED DOG DEACTIVATION

1. Stuart A. Mace, interview and transcript by Karen Fischer, Ashcroft CO, January 1982, S6/9.
2. Thomas R. Buecker, "Mules, Horses, and Dogs—Fort Robinson in World War II," *Council on Abandoned Military Posts, United States of America*, April 1989, 40.
3. Mace interview, S6/8.
4. "Lucky Was Worth $300," Associated Press clipping, newspaper and date unknown, Stuart A. Mace personal files.
5. Dick O'Malley, Associated Press news release, Camp Rimini, September 1943.
6. Mace interview, S7/6.
7. Mace interview, S7/5.
8. Buecker, "Mules, Horses, and Dogs," 46.
9. Stuart A. Mace, "Recollections of Stuart A. Mace, about His Army Service, the Tenth Mountain Division, and Military Dog Sledding," video interview by W. Michael Meyers, Snowmass CO, August 10, 1991.
10. Army Service Force, Office of the Quartermaster General, Washington DC, letter, July 20, 1945, Disposition of War Dogs.
11. Mace interview, S7/9.

6. SOLDIERS' SLEDS

1. War Department, *FM 25-6, Basic Field Manual, Dog Team Transportation* (Washington DC: War Department, January 4, 1941), 15–16.
2. War Department, *FM 25-6, 1941,* 17–20.
3. War Department, *FM 25-6, 1941,* 17–20.
4. War Department, *FM 25-6, 1941,* 17–20.
5. War Department, *FM 25-6, Dog Transportation,* (Washington DC: War Department, August 19, 1944), 10.
6. War Department, *FM 25-6, 1944,* 11–12.
7. War Department, *FM 25-6, 1944,* 12–13.
8. War Department, *FM 25-6, 1944.*
9. War Department, *FM 25-6, 1944,* 13–15.

10. War Department, *FM 25-6, 1944.*
11. War Department, *FM 25-6, 1944.*
12. David W. Armstrong Jr., letter to author, April 15, 1997.
13. Army Ground Forces, *History of the Mountain Training Center* (N.p., n.d.), Denver Public Library, Western History Department, 15.
14. Mountain and Winter Warfare Board, Camp Hale CO, letter and endorsements, To: Headquarters and Services Supply, Washington DC, March 5, 1943, Development Project, Sledge, Dog, 3rd Ind.
15. Stuart A. Mace, interview and transcript by Karen Fischer, Ashcroft CO, January 1982, S1/9.
16. Office of the Mountain and Winter Warfare Board, the Mountain Training Center, Camp Hale CO, report, May 10, 1943, To: Captain Richard Leonard, Office of the Quartermaster General, Washington DC.
17. Mountain and Winter Warfare Board, letter and endorsements, 11th Ind.
18. Office of the Winter Warfare Board, report, 2.
19. Office of the Quartermaster General, letter, To: Major Wendell M. Poulson Acting Director Executive, Mountain and Winter Warfare Board, Camp Hale CO, May 20, 1943, Convertible Sled-Toboggan.
20. John A. Matovich, letter to author, December 1996.
21. Matovich letter.
22. Matovich letter.
23. Mace interview, S7/6.
24. Mace interview, S3/6.
25. Matovich letter.
26. Mace interview, S6/8.
27. David W. Armstrong Jr., "World War II Memoirs" (unpublished), Helena MT, June 1997, 17.
28. Office of the Quartermaster General, Military Planning Division, Research and Development Branch, "Quartermaster Equipment on the Ronne Antarctic Research Expedition," May 1948, 73.

7. SLED DOGS SAVE LIVES

1. Brent Balchen, *Come North with Me* (New York: Dutton, 1958), 216.
2. Balchen, *Come North*, 218.
3. Norman D. Vaughn, *My Life of Adventure* (Mechanicsburg PA: Stackpole Books, 1995), 77.
4. Vaughn, *My Life of Adventure,* 74–79.
5. Brent Balchen, Corey Ford, and Oliver LaFarge, *War below Zero* (Boston: Houghton Mifflin, 1944).
6. Vaughn, *My Life of Adventure,* 96–100.

7. War Department, AG's Office, Washington DC, Letter 312, June 21, 1943, To: CG's, AAFTTC, Flight Control Command, "Construction and Activation of the First Arctic Search and Rescue Squadron."

8. C. B. Colby, "Men, Dogs, and Machines Save Flyers Who Crash in Arctic," *Popular Science* 147 (November 1945): 208.

9. War Department, *Table of Organization and Equipment No. 1–618* (Washington DC: War Department, September 15, 1943), 2.

10. War Department, *TOE No. 1–618*, 14.

11. War Department, *TOE No. 1–618*, 15.

12. War Department, *TOE No. 1–618*, 5.

13. War Department, *TOE No. 1–618*, 12.

14. David W. Armstrong Jr., letter to author, November 1996.

15. Dick Moulton, telephone interview with author, November 18, 1996.

16. David W. Armstrong Jr., "World War II Memoirs" (unpublished), Helena MT, June 1997, 86.

17. Armstrong memoirs, 62–71.

18. Norman D. Vaughn, letter to author, October 1996.

19. Ermond D. Hughes, "ATC Stages Spectacular Search, Rescue Drill in White Mountains," *Union* (Manchester NH), March 18, 1944, 1.

20. Vaughn, *My Life of Adventure*, 109–16.

21. Michael G. Lemish, *War Dogs: Canines in Combat* (Washington DC: Brassey's, 1996), 69.

22. "Famous Sled Drivers Rescue GI's in Belgium Snow," *Christian Science Monitor*, March 20, 1945, 1.

23. Vaughn, *My Life of Adventure*, 118.

24. Karen Fischer, "Training Sled Dogs at Camp Rimini, 1942–1944," *Montana, the Magazine of Western History* (Montana Historical Society, Helena) 34 (Winter 1984): 17.

25. Natalie Norris, "Reclamation Dogs and Men at Work," *Alaska Fur Rendezvous Annual*, 1956, 12.

26. Orvin L. Haugan, telephone interview with author, June 1997.

27. Eugene Armstrong, interview with author, Colorado Springs CO, June 1997.

28. Haugan interview.

29. Balchen, *Come North*, 303.

8. "GRRRONIMO!"

1. Stuart A. Mace, interview and transcript by Karen Fischer, Ashcroft CO, January 1982, S6/2.

2. Norman D. Vaughn, *My Life of Adventure* (Mechanicsburg PA: Stackpole Books, 1995), 122–25.

3. Norman D. Vaughn, telephone interview with author, September 16, 1996.

4. Mace interview, S6/2.

5. Mace interview, S6/3.

6. War Department, War Dog Reception and Training Center, Camp Rimini, Helena MT, letter with nine endorsements, To: Quartermaster General, War Department, Washington DC, ATTN: Remount Branch, 6th Ind., December 6, 1943, Parachute Harness for Dogs.

7. War Department, War Dog Reception and Training Center, Camp Rimini, Helena MT, report, March 24, 1944, Complete Description and Explanation of Rimini Dog Parachute Harness, 1.

8. War Department, letter with nine endorsements, 8th Ind.

9. Stuart A. Mace, "Recollections of Stuart A. Mace, about His Army Service, the Tenth Mountain Division, and Military Dog Sledding," video interview by W. Michael Meyers, Snowmass CO, August 10, 1991.

10. War Department, War Dog Reception and Training Center, Camp Rimini, Helena MT, report, April 4, 1944, Report of Parachuting Military Pack Dogs, 1–2.

11. War Department report, Parachuting Pack Dogs.

12. Mace interview, S6/5.

13. Mace interview, S6/5.

14. Pararescue Association of Canada, British Columbia, letter to author, December 19, 1997.

15. Phil Glanzer, "American Parapooches," *Our Dogs* 4, no. 1 (Fall 1945): 6–7.

16. Francis M. Dawdy, letter to author, May 20, 1997.

17. "Grrrronimo!" Flashback, *Air Force Magazine* 78, no. 3 (March 1995): 80.

18. *Pararescue, 50 Years, 1943–1993: A Commemorative History* (Dallas: Taylor, 1996).

19. Bud Selleck, *Skydiving: The Art and Science of Sport Parachuting* (Englewood Cliffs NJ: Prentice-Hall, 1961), 27–28.

20. Dawdy letter.

9. SLED DOGS IN SUMMER

1. War Department, War Dog Reception and Training Center, Helena MT, Memorandum 8, Sledge Dogs and Pack Dogs, September 30, 1943, 1.

2. War Department, memo, Sledge Dogs and Pack Dogs, 1.

3. War Department, *Basic Field Manual, Pack Dog Transportation*, draft manuscript, date unknown, 1, Stuart A. Mace personal files.

4. War Department, War Dog Reception and Training Center, Camp Rimini, Helena MT, Special Orders 130, December 10, 1943, 2.

5. David W. Armstrong Jr., "World War II Memoirs" (unpublished), Helena MT, June 1997, 13.

6. Stuart A. Mace, interview and transcript by Karen Fischer, Ashcroft CO, January 1982, S5/1–3.
7. Army Service Forces, Quartermaster Corps, War Dog Reception and Training Center, Camp Rimini, Helena, Montana, letter, To: Quartermaster General, War Department, ATTN: SPQOR, Major Strawbridge, March 30, 1944, Types of Military Pack Dogs, 1.
8. Army Service Forces letter.
9. Armstrong memoir, 62.
10. Army Service Forces letter, 2.
11. War Department, draft manuscript, 2–3.
12. War Department, draft manuscript, 3.
13. Mace interview, S5/1–3.
14. Dick O'Malley, Associated Press news release, Camp Rimini, September 1943.
15. Mace interview, S5/1–3.
16. War Department, draft manuscript, 4.
17. Mace interview, S5/6.
18. War Department, draft manuscript, 4.
19. War Department, draft manuscript, 4.
20. Army Service Forces letter, 1–2.
21. Mace interview, S4/9.
22. O'Malley news release.
23. War Department, draft manuscript, 15–17.
24. War Department, draft manuscript.
25. War Department, draft manuscript, 19–21.
26. Mace interview, S5/4.
27. War Department, War Dog Reception and Training Center, Camp Rimini, Helena MT, report, Dog Packs, July 31, 1943.
28. War Department, draft manuscript, 11–14.
29. Mace interview, S5/7.
30. Hazzard H. Ruland, letter to Lt. Stuart A. Mace, March 19, 1944.

10. SLED DOGS AND THE SS

1. Otto Schulz, letter to author, February 1997.
2. James Lucas, *Hitler's Mountain Troops* (London: Arms and Armour Press, 1992), 109.
3. Schulz letter.
4. War Department, Military Intelligence Division, *German Ski Training and Tactics*, Special Series 20 (Washington DC: War Department, January 31, 1944), 87–88.

5. War Department, Military Intelligence Division, *German Winter Warfare*, Special Series 18 (Washington DC: War Department, December 1943), 198–200.
6. Schulz letter.
7. Schulz letter.
8. Schulz letter.
9. Lucas, *Hitler's Mountain Troops*, 203.
10. Schulz letter.
11. Schulz letter.
12. Richard S. Moulton, telephone interview with author, November 18, 1996.
13. Lucas, *Hitler's Mountain Troops*.
14. Schulz letter.

11. DOG TEAM DÉJÀ VU

1. Judy Ferguson, "Put to the Test," *Heartland Magazine, Fairbanks AK Daily News-Miner,* January 19, 1997, printed from the Internet April 1, 1999 (www.newsminer.com/heartland/hland/1997/army.html), 1.
2. Department of the Army, FM 31–7, *Northern Operations* (Washington DC, June 21, 1971), 1–2.
3. Ferguson, "Put to the Test," 1.
4. Ferguson, "Put to the Test," 1.
5. Jesse Taylor, taped interview by Judy Ferguson, Fairbanks AK, 1996.
6. Ferguson, "Put to the Test," 2.
7. Taylor interview.
8. Ferguson, "Put to the Test," 3.
9. Taylor interview.
10. Ferguson, "Put to the Test," 2.
11. Department of the Army, FM 31-7, *Basic Cold Weather Manual* (Washington DC, April 12, 1968), 119–20.
12. Ferguson, "Put to the Test," 2.
13. Taylor interview.
14. Marcello Diaz Lastra, LTC, Argentine Embassy, Military Attaché's Office, 1810 Connecticut Avenue NW, Washington DC, letter to the author, April 9, 1999.
15. Ferguson, "Put to the Test."
16. Taylor interview.
17. Ferguson, "Put to the Test."
18. Ferguson, "Put to the Test."
19. Ferguson, "Put to the Test."
20. Taylor interview.

21. John R. Callahan (former army instructor at Arctic Indoctrination Center), Delta Junction AK, telephone interview with author, April 5, 1999.

12. SLED DOGS AND SECRET SURVEILLANCE

1. Brent Balchen, *Come North with Me* (New York: Dutton, 1958), 247.
2. Balchen, *Come North*, 248.
3. *Sledge Patrol SIRIUS*, Commander, Patrol Branch, North and Northeast Greenland, 1999, 3.
4. Balchen, *Come North*, 248–52.
5. *Sledge Patrol SIRIUS*, 3–4.
6. Poul Ipsen, Mestersvig, Greenland, letter to author, October 12, 1998.
7. *Sledge Patrol SIRIUS*, 1, 4.
8. *Sledge Patrol SIRIUS*, 4–5.
9. Peter Schmidt Mikkelsen, e-mail to author, January 9, 1999.
10. *Sledge Patrol SIRIUS*, 6.
11. Poul Ipsen, Mestersvig, Greenland, letter to author, May 19, 1999.
12. Ipsen letter.
13. Carsten Nielsen and Henrik Lassen, "SIRIUS," *Royal Danish Newsletter* (Royal Danish Embassy, London), April 13, 1998.
14. Ipsen letter, May 19, 1999.
15. Mikkelsen e-mail.
16. Ipsen letter, May 19, 1999.
17. Ipsen letter, May 19, 1999.
18. Ipsen letter, May 19, 1999.
19. Ipsen letter, May 19, 1999.
20. *Sledge Patrol SIRIUS*, 7.
21. Nielsen and Lassen, "SIRIUS."
22. *Sledge Patrol SIRIUS*, 6–7.
23. Mikkelsen e-mail.
24. Ipsen letter, May 19, 1999.

Bibliography

Army, Department of the. *FM-31-70, Basic Cold Weather Manual.* Washington DC:
    Department of the Army, April 12, 1968.
————. *FM 31-71, Northern Operations,* Washington DC: Department of the Army,
    June 21, 1971.
Army Ground Forces. *History of the Mountain Training Center.* N.p., n.d.
Balchen, Brent. *Come North with Me.* New York: Dutton, 1958.
Balchen, Brent, Corey Ford, and Oliver Lafarge. *War below Zero.* Boston:
    Houghton Mifflin, 1944.
Brearley, Joan McDonald. *This Is the Siberian Husky.* Neptune City NJ: T.F.S., 1974.
Buecker, Thomas R. "Mules, Horses and Dogs—Fort Robinson in World War II."
    Council on Abandoned Military Posts, United States of America, April
    1989, 34–49.
Cellura, Dominique. *Travelers of the Cold: Sled Dogs of the Far North.* Anchorage:
    Alaska Northwest Books, 1989.
Colby, C. B. "Men, Dogs, and Machines Save Flyers Who Crash in
    Arctic." *Popular Science* 147 (November 1945): 122–27, 208.
"Famous Sled Drivers Rescue Wounded GI's in Belgium Snow." *Christian Science
    Monitor,* March 20, 1945.
Ferguson, Judy. "Put to the Test." *Heartland Magazine, Fairbanks AK Daily
    News-Miner,* January 19, 1997. Printed from the Internet April 1, 1999.
    www.newsminer.com/heartland/hland/1997/army.html.
Fischer, Karen. "Training Sled Dogs at Camp Rimini, 1942–1944." *Montana, the
    Magazine of Western History* (Montana Historical Society, Helena) 34
    (Winter 1984): 10–19.
France, Ministère de la Défense. "Tot Dret." *Bulletin d'Information de l'École
    Militaire de Haute Montagne* (Chamonix), n.d.
Garst, Shannon. *Scotty Allan, King of the Dog Team Drivers.* New York: Julian
    Messner, 1946.
Glanzer, Phil. "American Parapooches." *Our Dogs* 4, no. 1 (Fall 1945): 6–7.
Gregory, Barry. *Mountain and Arctic Warfare: From Alexander to Afghanistan.*
    Wellingborough, Eng.: Patrick Stephens, 1989.

"Grrrronimo!" Flashback. *Air Force Magazine* 78, no. 3 (March 1995): 80.

Howarth, David. *The Sledge Patrol*. New York: Macmillan, 1957.

Hughes, Ermond D. "ATC Stages Spectacular Search, Rescue Drill in White Mountains." *Union* (Manchester NH), March 18, 1944, 1, 9.

Khatchikan, Ararad. "Sled Dogs Do Their Part in World War I." *Mushing* 35 (November–December 1993): 29.

Lemish, Michael G. *War Dogs: Canines in Combat*. Washington DC: Brussey's, 1996.

Lucas, James. *Hitler's Mountain Troops*. London: Arms and Armour Press, 1992.

"Lucky Was Worth $300." Associated Press clipping, newspaper and date unknown. Stuart A. Mace personal files.

Nelson, Jerry Ray. "Blazer of Trails." *Mushing* 67 (March–April 1999): 21–22.

"New England Sled Dog Club History." Fiftieth anniversary club booklet (1974). Printed from the Internet June 1999. www.gsinet.net/~blackrvr/history.htm.

Nielsen, Carsten, and Henry Lassen. "SIRIUS." *Royal Danish Newsletter* (Royal Danish Embassy, London), April 13, 1998.

Norris, Natalie. "Reclamation Dogs and Men at Work." In *Alaska Fur Rendezvous Annual*, 12. Anchorage AK, 1956.

O'Malley, Dick. Associated Press news release. Camp Rimini, September 1943.

Pararescue, 50 Years, 1943–1993: A Commemorative History. Dallas: Taylor, 1996.

Selleck, Bud. *Skydiving: The Art and Science of Sport Parachuting*. Englewood Cliffs NJ: Prentice-Hall, 1961.

Sledge Patrol SIRIUS. Commander, Patrol Branch, North and Northeast Greenland, 1999.

"Training Dogs for War." *Mountain Bell Magazine*, 1942, 4, 5.

Vaughn, Norman D. *My Life of Adventure*. Mechanicsburg PA: Stackpole Books, 1995.

War Department. FM 25-6, *Basic Field Manual, Dog Team Transportation*. Washington DC: War Department, January 4, 1941.

———. FM 25-6, *Dog Transportation*. Washington DC: War Department, August 19, 1944.

———. FM 70-15, *Operations in Snow and Extreme Cold*. War Department, November 1944.

———. *Table of Organization and Equipment, No. 1–618, Army Air Forces, Arctic Search and Rescue Squadron, Flight Control Command*. Washington DC: War Department, September 15, 1943.

———. *Technical Regulation No. 1380-20, Dog Transportation*. Washington DC: War Department, June 15, 1926.

War Department, Military Intelligence Division. *German Winter Warfare.* Special
    Series 18. Washington DC: War Department, December 1943.
————. *German Ski Training and Tactics.* Special Series 20. Washington DC: War
    Department, January 31, 1944.
Viazzi, Luciano. "Guerra 1915–18: Sull'Adamello i cani da traino." *Alpino,* 1986,
    26–29.

Index